CURRENT AFRICAN ISSUES 59

Resettled for Development
The Case of New Halfa Agricultural Scheme, Sudan

Marianna Wallin

(M.Sc., University of Helsinki)

NORDISKA AFRIKAINSTITUTET, UPPSALA 2014

INDEXING TERMS:
Sudan, New Halfa
Agricultural development
Resettlement
Irrigation
Living conditions
Nubians
Pastoralists
Nomads

The opinions expressed in this volume are those of the author
and do not necessarily reflect the views of the Nordic Africa Institute.

ISSN 0280-2171
ISBN 978-91-7106-751-7
Language editing: Peter Colenbrander
© The author and the Nordic Africa Institute
Production: Byrå4
Print on demand, Lightning Source UK Ltd.

Contents

Abstract 4

1. Introduction 5

2. Dams as catalysts for development: Hydraulic engineering in Sudan 10

3. The changing agricultural landscapes of Sudan 14

4. Development perspectives 17
   4.1 Displacement for development 17
   4.2 Resettlement consequences 18
   4.3 Land rights and territorialisation 20
   4.4 Social consequences of dams' construction and irrigation schemes 21

5. The transforming sense of national identity in Sudan 24
   5.1 The Nubians of Wadi Halfa 25
   5.2 Sacrifices of land and identity 27

6. Study Area; the New Halfa Agricultural Scheme 29
   6.1 The town of New Halfa and the surrounding villages 31
   6.2 The ethnic composition of New Halfa today 32
   6.3 Changes and challenges in New Halfa 36
   6.4 Social consequences of the resettlement of the Halfawi Nubians 38
   6.5 Sedentarisation of pastoral nomads in New Halfa region 39

7. For better or for worse; New Halfa today from the residents' perspective 42
   7.1 Present conditions and challenges for the farmer in New Halfa 42
   7.2 Other livelihood means and income sources 43
   7.3 Quality of water and environmental changes 46
   7.4 Housing, infrastructure and services 48
   7.5 Equality and integration 50

8. Victims or beneficiaries of development? 53
   8.1 New Halfa as a showcase of resettlement of the Halfawi Nubians 55
   8.2 The situation of the nomadic groups in New Halfa 57
   8.3 Future prospects for New Halfa and Sudanese agriculture 59

9. Conclusion 61

References 63

Abstract

This paper discusses the displacement and resettlement of the Sudanese Nubians into the New Halfa agricultural scheme in Eastern Sudan, the current state of this multi-ethnic community and the challenges the farmers are facing. The Nubians of Wadi Halfa in Northern Sudan (also called the *Halfawi* Nubians) had to be relocated to New Halfa due to the construction of the Aswan High Dam in the early 1960s. In addition to the loss of ancestral land and the alienation they experienced, the Halfawi Nubians struggled to secure a sufficient livelihood in New Halfa and found their lives irreversibly altered. Furthermore, the lives of the local nomadic groups of the New Halfa region had to be adjusted and some of them were incorporated into the scheme as farmers. The vast economic and social differences between the compensated resettled Nubians and the host population of nomads and migrant workers led to fragmentation and resentment among the different ethnic groups. The forced displacement and resettlement failed to create permanent social development and the current self-determined farming practices and supplementing occupations of the residents are the determining factors for the sustainability of the scheme. Although the resettlement of the Nubians did not succeed in rooting them in their new territory and a lot of the Halfawi Nubians have since abandoned the scheme, New Halfa has also created unforeseen opportunities for internally displaced people and migrant workers and become a growing regional centre for business and commerce. Despite the fact that New Halfa failed to meet its original targets, it is an example of a resettlement scheme that, in 50 years, developed and adjusted according to the needs of its current inhabitants. With sufficient social impact assessment and the active participation of the resettled people and host population some of the current challenges could have been mitigated.

1. Introduction

In this paper I will discuss the displacement and the resettlement of the Nubians of Wadi Halfa, in Northern Sudan, into the new Halfa agricultural scheme in the 1960s. The purpose of this paper is to look into the scheme's current situation and to look at how the various ethnic groups within New Halfa, including the Nubians, have managed to settle and secure a living from this agricultural scheme. The information for this paper was gathered during field work in New Halfa in July-August 2011 where interviews and group discussions were held with members of different communities within the scheme. Additional information has also been gathered from research conducted at New Halfa prior to 2011 and from various secondary sources.

In July 2011, after decades of on-going power imbalances and political conflict, South Sudan seceded from Sudan and became a newly independent country. The situation at the New Halfa Agricultural Scheme, in Eastern Sudan, however was calm and the turmoil at the border between these suddenly new neighbours did not have much affect on the everyday life of this agricultural community. The secession of South Sudan was a result of endless conflict over politics, power, rights to natural resources and the unresolved differences between North and South Sudan. Although the situation of South Sudan did not directly touch the communities in New Halfa, the same underlying issues of political power and access to resources have also extensively affected the current state of the New Halfa scheme.

The country of Sudan, situated in the northeast of Africa, is well known through global media for its political instabilities, poverty and harsh climate. The ethnic and cultural richness and the significant environmental resources are thus overshadowed by the continuing flow of negative news from the country. Nevertheless, Sudan is a country of diversity and complexity when it comes to geography, politics, culture and religion. Although South Sudan officially declared its independence on 9th July 2011, Sudan still remains the third largest country in Africa (UNDP Sudan 2013). The conflicts in Sudan cannot be blamed only on its ethnic diversity, poverty or the geographical size of the country. Throughout its history Sudan has faced various eras of foreign and biased rule, and that has justified the legitimacy of political power resting with a chosen few. This has arranged the ethnic fabric in such a way that some have claimed more political power at the expense of others. As a consequence the history and the landscape have been reshaped by the political power elite and the ethnic minorities have had to choose between submission and existence on the periphery.

One of the apparent manifestations of power was the construction of dams and the transformation of rural landscape. Although Sudan was in the wake of Egypt when it came to modernisation, gaining independence in 1956 pushed

Sudan towards further development and economic growth. Unarguably the construction of dams brought development through water control, electricity and irrigation possibilities. They were also visible symbols of national growth and might. However, the downside of these development initiatives was the destruction of cultural heritage sites and the forced relocation of thousands of people off their traditional homeland. This was a high cost to those who, already marginalised, had to step aside and compromise their livelihoods. This became a reality during the construction of the Aswan High Dam along the River Nile in Southern Egypt, that forced the relocation of thousands of Nubians off their traditional land, both in Egypt and in Sudan. Although the construction of the Aswan High Dam was an Egyptian initiative, the Nubian resettlement that followed was incorporated into the Sudanese development plan of agricultural intensification and nationalisation. This manifested itself in the establishment of the New Halfa agricultural scheme that was to settle the Nubians and local nomadic groups into an irrigation scheme in Eastern Sudan.

The more recent, extensive dam constructions in Sudan – the Merowe Dam and the Kajbar Dam – have continued to displace thousands of communities away from their traditional land (International Rivers Network 2013). It is primarily the poor and marginal people who are forced to sacrifice their lifestyles and traditions, for the sake of modernity and growth, without adequate compensation for their losses. Therefore these mega-scale development initiatives represent a one-sided view of progress. This nation building and modernisation that took place in Sudan also enforced the mainstreaming of the Sudanese nation and economy. This happened at the expense of minor ethnic groups such as the Nubians and the nomadic groups on the peripheries. The top-down view on development may not correspond to the views of the people affected when it is changing their lifestyle against their wishes.

In Sudan today one may still come across isolated desert regions with sporadic nomad communities continuing their traditional lifestyles, in contrast to the massive irrigation schemes creating products for the global market. However, the increasing agricultural development has come at a cost. The development of agricultural schemes and the construction of large dams have collided with the more traditional lifestyles of subsistence farming and pastoralism. Many nomads have had to change their pastoral routes due to the irrigation schemes and settle for marginal land. The construction of dams has forced large populations to relocate to foreign areas and adapt to new methods of more mechanised agriculture.

In spite of this, this hydraulic engineering is enabling the kind of development that will boost the economy and overall national growth that Sudan needs. The development of modern agriculture in Sudan has been made possible with the harnessing of the Nile waters and by altering traditional livelihoods. Today, agriculture makes up a third of the economic sector in Sudan. Cash crops such as cotton and gum arabic are the cornerstones of Sudanese agricultural export. However, problems of irrigation, technical maintenance, environmental degradation and poor transportation remain the greatest constraints to the growth of the Sudanese agricultural sector (UNDP Sudan 2013). Due to financial difficulties and lack of efficient natural resource management many agricultural schemes are now facing loss of land fertility and productivity. For an average farmer, the income from an agricultural scheme is not sufficient and many are migrating to Khartoum in the hope of more urban employment. The division between the Sudanese core and periphery, both geographically and socially, seems to grow deeper. The development-induced displacement of people and the construction of irrigation schemes are still continuing, despite the unresolved challenges of the existing schemes. People in the schemes lack social cohesion and often feel rootless in their new surroundings. The privatisation and neoliberalism that have reached the schemes are placing the farmers under pressure to produce more out of the deteriorating environment.

The particular case of the New Halfa agricultural scheme is interesting as it is one of the oldest schemes in Sudan and was the destination of one of the largest population resettlement projects in the history of the country. Yet it has been facing both external and internal pressure to meet the standards that were set out for it. The scheme has been running for almost 50 years and the loss of productivity, insufficiency of the infrastructure and environmental degradation are easy to see. The Khasm el Girba dam that feeds the water to the scheme has become sedimented thus reducing its capacity to distribute water. The existing service sector has not been expanded sufficiently to accommodate the natural population growth in the scheme and the residents have had to turn to additional means of living, as the income from farming is not satisfactory. The declining rates of production and increasing environmental degradation are causing a headache for the farmers and some are looking into other sources of livelihood. The scheme consists of different ethnic groups that are facing different challenges and circumstances. Originally the New Halfa scheme was planned for the Halfawi Nubians that were resettled due to the construction of the Aswan High Dam. It attempted to remould the existing social composition by incorporating the detached Nubians and the self-sufficient nomads into a new social system of tenancy and intensive farming. New Halfa became a melting pot for different ethnic groups from varying socio-economic backgrounds (Dafalla 1975). One of the key challenges facing the scheme, right from the start, has been the inequality between the different communities, which has differentiated and fragmented the scheme. This has evidently had a negative effect on the social cohesion of the scheme. Some farmers have managed to accumulate farmland and hire farm labour while pursuing other careers, in contrast to other residents who are dependent on any work they can find on a daily basis (Sørbø 1985). Therefore, some of the first irrigation schemes in Sudan, such as New Halfa, have become crucial focal points as they give an opportunity to observe the evolution of the state controlled agricultural schemes towards the more neo-liberal and differentiated schemes they are today. The challenges these schemes are facing have not gone unnoticed. However, little has been done to solve these problems while new resettlements and agricultural schemes are being initiated.

Taking the example of New Halfa, this study looks at the impacts of large-scale schemes and top-down development initiatives on the grassroots level in the context of a developing country like Sudan. It is particularly relevant today as new dams are being built in the northern parts of Sudan, which forces communities to resettle in other areas, commonly into irrigation schemes. The instability of Sudanese politics, the changing economic landscape and increasing urbanisation have all had an effect on the development of the agricultural sector. There is a need to find out whether these agricultural schemes have been conducive to overall rural development and are sustainable in the long run. What is the current definition of a state driven irrigation scheme that was also designed as a resettlement project, almost 50 years after it was established? The legacy of the Nubian resettlement, sedentarisation of the nomads, and the influx of internal refugees from Western Sudan have all influenced the development of the scheme and created increasing social differentiation due to different economic backgrounds. Local opinions about the scheme are particularly relevant as the future prospects of these schemes relies strongly on the choices and interests of the farmers and local residents. The sustainability of the ecosystem, the sufficiency of the Nile waters and the sense of purpose and future optimism of the farmers are the components that define the future of the Sudanese agricultural schemes.

The example of the New Halfa agricultural scheme could give a valuable insight into the relocation process and the sustainability of agricultural schemes. However, as new agricultural schemes are being established in Sudan, the current deteriorating state of the older schemes receives little attention. The recent droughts seen in East Africa and the increasing environmental degradation and climate change will further increase the demand for natural resources. Furthermore, the political power struggle to decide over the utilisation of natural resources will become even more agitated. The shift from food crop production towards cash crop production has made the Sudanese agricultural industry more dependent on global price fluctuations and placed the local farmer in a more vulnerable position.

The varying degrees of social differentiation and inequality between the different ethnic groups in New Halfa show the failure of the scheme to operate with the principle of equal sized tenancies. The resettled Halfawi's lack of attachment to, and ownership of, the scheme and the failure to successfully incorporate the nomadic pastoralists into a stationary agricultural lifestyle are also results of poor social planning by the scheme. The poor state of agricultural resources, lack of services and deteriorating environment are also push-factors for people leaving the scheme. This can be set against the overall attempt of the Sudanese government to mainstream the Sudanese nation and to uniform the existing traditional lifestyles into a more modern capitalist economy. However, the aim of this study is not to decide whether the New Halfa scheme was a failure that should have been avoided or a success of agricultural development. Rather, I want to bring forward the pitfalls and risks of using resettlement as a means for development, and the challenges that must be considered in the planning. Also, local opinions will be relevant as future planning of resettlement and agricultural development will need a greater contribution from – and empowerment of – the people actually involved.

2. Dams as catalysts for development: Hydraulic engineering in Sudan

The source of the River Nile lies in the Great Lakes region in central Africa and in the Ethiopian highlands. There, the White and the Blue Nile tributaries start to twist their way down and finally merge together in Khartoum to become the great River Nile. Nearly 80 % of Sudan lies within the Nile basin, making it the most important source of freshwater in Sudan. Sudan (including South Sudan) has a total natural renewable water resource of 149 km^3/year, of which 20 % is from rainfall and 80 % from the Nile water flows from upstream countries such as Ethiopia (UNEP 2007). The River Nile is a natural process that is constantly altering its surrounding environment and influencing the biophysical ecosystems it flows through. It has provided opportunities for sustainable human settlement and agriculture for over 7,000 years (Chesworth 1990). Throughout history people have looked for various ways to benefit from the river, thus a relationship between the environment and society has always existed. However, following the expansion of the human population and settlements around the Nile river valley, the need for industrialisation and irrigated agriculture has subsequently increased. This has resulted in a growing demand for alterations and harnessing of the River Nile. The physical environment is changing through the increasing socio-political actions of dam construction, agricultural schemes, industrialisation and overall human utilisation of natural resources (Swyngedouw 2009; Minoia 2012).

Hydraulic engineering is a necessary part of the overall development of a country and its growing population. Some of the first dams in the world were built in the Middle East in 3000 BC and dams were used for hydropower generation for the first time in 1890. In the 20th century the construction of dams boomed and by the end of the century there were over 45,000 large dams worldwide (World Commission on Dams 2000). In Africa the construction of large hydroelectric dams has been a trend in development initiatives since the early 20th century. Between 1945 and 1990 over a thousand large dams of at least 15 metres in height have been built in Africa, providing over 22 percent of Africa's electricity (Hoag 2013).

For many developing countries with a history of colonial rule, gaining independence and decolonisation became the political engines for constructing megaprojects such as dams. In Egypt, and to some extent in Sudan, hydroelectric development and the construction of large irrigation schemes was a necessary step in meeting the needs of the growing nation and economy. New leaders of newly independent developing countries such as Nasser, Nkrumah and Nehru were all striving for the positive symbolism of dams and geographic engineering. They were also necessary technological advancements that further developed the irrigated agriculture sector and provided power for the growing economy.

Therefore, besides their pragmatic purpose, the constructions served as concrete examples of modernity, prosperity and autonomy (Collins 2008; Nixon 2010).

The hydraulic engineering in Sudan was primarily established by the British in order to increase and secure the flow of the Nile waters in Egypt. Sudan was ruled as a condominium by Britain and Egypt from 1899 until independence in 1956 (Taha 2010:186). The first official agreement over the utilisation of the Nile waters between Egypt and Sudan was made in 1929, when the Anglo-Egyptian Waters Agreement gave Egypt a lion's share of the Nile waters. However, when Egypt was planning the Aswan High Dam, Sudan's population had almost doubled since 1929 and it was in dire need of a larger share of the waters (Taha 2010:187). As a result of long discussions, Sudan and Egypt signed the revised Nile Waters Agreement of 1959 that increased the water shares for both countries (Collins 1990). The agreement also settled the compensation for Sudan over the construction of the Aswan High Dam in Egypt that led to the inundation of the Sudanese Nubia (Taha 2010:190). Although the local consequences of the building of the Aswan High Dam were socially disastrous for the Nubians, it gave Egypt the necessary water and power to support its vision of development and much needed growth of the agricultural sector.

Hydrological development such as constructing dams, reservoirs, canals or power plants often comes with the cost of negative social and environmental consequences such as environmental degradation, social resettlement and loss of traditional and cultural land (Staddon 1988). The aquatic ecosystem may face negative impacts due to the changes in the water flow and in the inundated area, silt and debris is deposited and aquatic weeds start to build up. In addition, the large water reservoirs cause higher evaporation in arid regions (Omer 2007). The construction of megaprojects, such as the Aswan High Dam between Sudan and Egypt or the Three Gorges Dam in China, has already resulted in serious consequences for the local residents and the surrounding environment. Generally, besides the negative consequences in the socio-physical environment, the dam constructions have resulted in even more economic and political indebtedness of the developing countries to the first and second worlds (Nixon 2010).

The United Nations Environment Programme completed an environmental assessment in Sudan in 2007 and also inspected all of the existing dams. Unarguably, the benefits of the dams in Sudan could be seen through electricity creation and irrigation. However, many negative environmental impacts were also detected (UNEP 2007). All of the dams visited had performance problems and visible environmental problems. Upstream land degradation caused sediment deposition and loss of reservoir capacity; and downstream impacts, due to water diversion and changes in the flow regime, were detected. For instance, the Khasm el Girba dam that supports the New Halfa scheme had lost up to 54 % of the original capacity since the year of commissioning in 1964 (UNEP 2007).

However, the construction of the Tekeze dam in Ethiopia in 2009 has since resulted in the reduction of the sedimentation of the Khasm el Girba reservoir.

Hydraulic engineering is continuing to alter the environment in Sudan, as the need for natural resources and the desire for economic growth sees no end. Other countries, such as China, have also begun to show interest in sharing in the opportunities of the Nile basin. The most recent addition to Sudanese dams, the Merowe dam below the fourth cataract of the Nile, is Sudan's largest construction project to date. It is estimated that the construction cost up to 2 billion US dollars and it has been partly funded by China's Exim Bank, several Arab funds, and partly by the Sudanese government's national budget for development (Jok 2007; Cockett 2010). The Merowe dam is meant to benefit the whole country, through electricity, employment and agricultural development. It will roughly double Sudan's power supply and will help irrigate land that is now barely arable. It has even been seen as the symbol of Sudan's future (Jok 2007). However, at the moment it is only benefiting a limited area of Sudan and some of the negative aspects of the dam are the forced evacuation and resettlement of thousands of people (Jok 2007; UNEP 2007; Cockett 2010). A full and transparent environmental, economic and social impact assessment has not been conducted and the positive and negative features of the project have not been widely discussed (UNEP 2007). Criticism of the project has been strong both internally and internationally, and the International Rivers Network and the Corner House published a report complaining about the false promises and non-existant services promised for the people being relocated as a result of the project (Jok 2007). The Nubian people in particular complain that the development and industrialisation of Sudan is being carried out at the expense of their heritage and dignity (Jok 2007).

Despite the negative consequences, the necessity and benefits of hydro-engineering must also be stated. With the Nile basin being partly situated in one of the world's most arid regions with a rapidly growing population, the need for securing food and energy supply is top priority. For many African countries the construction of dams is one of the few feasible options (Oestigaard 2012). Naturally there are many economic benefits to hydro-engineering. It makes it possible to regulate the flow of water to control flooding, to generate power and to channel water for irrigation purposes (Oestigaard 2012). For many nations and regions, these megaprojects are also a way of creating employment, advancing technology and producing a concrete symbol for national development and pride (Staddon 1988). Some developing countries have also seen the construction of megaprojects such as hydraulic dams or irrigation schemes as concrete evidence of catching up with the developed world and showcasing the technological advancements and development of the country (Nixon 2010).

It must also be acknowledged that the need for dam construction is considerable. The current power generation in Sudan is lagging behind demand. The feasibility of dams for energy production is clear and there are many potential sites for hydropower generation on the main Nile and its tributaries (Omer 2007). Despite the fact that the construction of dams is a controversial topic that evokes strong opinions for and against, the common consent is that their benefits outweigh the negative consequences. It is, however, important to consider the environmental and socio-economic issues and carry out impact and risk assessments as well as pre-feasibility studies (Gourbesville 2008). Although the social implications of dam construction and irrigation schemes have been academically discussed, it has not had much impact on the policies of hydro engineering. Even the most recent dam constructions have not succeeded in mitigating the negative social and environmental consequences. Furthermore, the maintenance of the old irrigation projects tends to be put to one side. The Gezira Scheme, being the largest irrigation scheme in the world, and the New Halfa Scheme the second largest in Sudan, have struggled to keep up with production targets, mitigate environmental problems and provide a stable income for the farmers (Haydar 2008).

3. The changing agricultural landscapes of Sudan

Agriculture has long been the backbone of the Sudanese economy (Sørbø 1985; NHAPC 2011). In the beginning of the 20th century agricultural schemes started to emerge around the River Nile and its tributaries and irrigated agriculture increased as cash crops such as cotton, sugar cane and wheat started to bring in revenue through foreign trade (Abdelrazig 1979). Today Sudan has the second greatest irrigated area in Africa after Egypt (Taha 2010: 179). A large share of the first irrigation schemes in Sudan were started by the British colonial administration for cash crop production and export purposes. The first of these was the Sennar Dam built in 1925 along the Blue Nile in order to water the great Gezira Scheme and enable cotton production (Taha 2010: 183).

However, before long the agricultural sector began to face challenges of increasing environmental degradation, insecurities of global market prices and the emerging conflicts within Sudan. Population is growing, yields are declining and the environment is deteriorating. While most of the agricultural schemes in the country are focusing on the farming of export crops for revenue, according to UNEP at least 15 % of the population is dependent on imported food aid (UNEP 2007). The Sudan Comprehensive National Strategy for the Agricultural Sector (1992–2002) identified the main targets on its agenda as food security, sustainable agricultural development, efficient resource utilisation and yield enhancement. With the necessary maintenance and management the agricultural sector in Sudan could turn the negative prospects around. However, these targets have not been successfully met. Even more discouraging is the fact that very little has been done to improve the accessibility of food to the poor and marginalised and more focus has been placed on cash crops (Omer 2007).

Approximately 40 % of the land area in Sudan is cultivable (UNEP 2007). There are five main types of farming practised in Sudan; mechanised rain-fed agricultural schemes, traditional rain-fed agriculture, mechanised irrigation schemes, traditional irrigation and livestock husbandry/pastoralism (UNEP 2007). The irrigation schemes are further divided into two categories; the Nile flood and pump schemes, and the national irrigation schemes such as Gezira, Rahad, New Halfa and Suki which constitute over 60 per cent of the total irrigated area (Haydar 2008). These schemes are the four largest national schemes in the country and consume 60 % of the current Sudanese annual water abstraction (See figure 1.) (Omer 2007). The most important local food crops that are grown on the schemes are maize, groundnuts, sugar cane and sorghum. Since the times of British colonialism the growth of cotton and other cash crops such as gum arabic, sesame and groundnuts have been promoted for export purposes (UNEP 2007). To a large extent the growth of cash crops is still promoted by the Sudanese government.

After gaining independence Sudan wanted to increase agricultural production by expanding irrigated areas, mechanisation, rain-fed agriculture and promoting efficiency. However, although Sudan's irrigated agriculture has been its most important economic investment, many studies have shown that its performance has been below expectations (UNEP 2007). Although the Gezira is still the largest irrigation scheme in the world, it has turned out to have a general irrigation efficiency of less than 50 per cent. The farmers cannot earn a satisfactory income from their crops and the siltation in the canals has caused parts of the scheme to be without sufficient irrigation water (Government of Sudan and the World Bank 2000). The Gezira scheme is not an exception and the situation of many irrigation schemes, such as New Halfa, portrays a gloomy picture at present. In many agricultural schemes siltation in the canals has increased thus

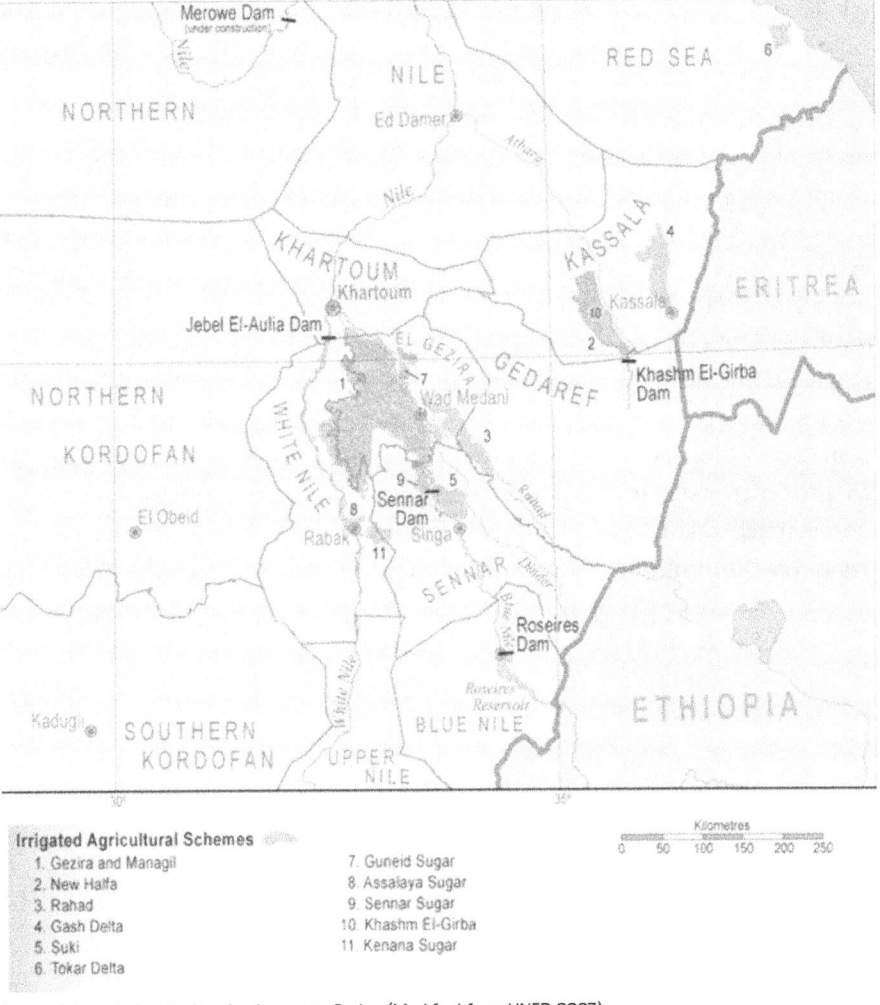

Figure 1. Irrigated agricultural schemes in Sudan (Modified from UNEP 2007).

decreasing the storage capacity of water, land fertility has decreased and equipment has become outdated (Omer 2007).

Nevertheless, irrigation schemes have long been a strong part of the Sudanese economy and continue to be so. There is no lack of arable land or absolute water scarcity in Sudan, but the challenge is the maintenance of the schemes, the irrigation systems and bringing enough profit to the farmers. Most of the irrigation schemes were started as parastatal establishments but since Sudan adopted a free market economy, privatisation and decentralisation system, the aim is to turn the schemes into private, financially independent corporations. Farmers' associations should have the upper hand in the funding and management and the communities should take more responsibility. Furthermore, agricultural co-operatives and the private sector are encouraged to operate the schemes (Omer 2007). Clearly the crop price fluctuations, decreasing land fertility and problems related to irrigation and agriculture infrastructure have made this goal impossible to reach. Most schemes continue to depend upon the state for financial support.

Irrigated agriculture has been a major source of employment for Sudanese people, but the challenge is to bring the farmer enough income to be able to focus solely on this livelihood and not be forced to look for additional sources of income. As with many other countries in Africa, Sudan is also dependent on export revenues from cash crops. The changing global economy, environmental degradation and the on-going political conflicts have also had negative effects on the agricultural sector. Sudan is facing high levels of urbanisation and many traditional nomadic groups are sedentarised and incorporated into the mainstream Sudanese economy. This will eventually change the social rural landscape and ultimately affect the sustainability of Sudan's agricultural schemes. In a seminar on environment, climate and the Sudanese conflicts, Gunnar M. Sørbø stated that Sudan is suffering from a crisis of livelihoods and governance. The shift from subsistence agriculture to mechanised agricultural schemes has dispossessed many local farmers and pastoralists of their customary rights (Sørbø 2012). In times of climate change, increasing food demand and the shift to cash crop farming, the conflicts over land rights and between different livelihoods may increase.

4. Development perspectives

Resettlement as a development initiative has been widely debated and regarded as a necessary sacrifice for the sake of long-term development. This paper discusses the effectiveness of resettlement as a development strategy and its success in terms of social integration and cultural adaptation in the New Halfa resettlement scheme. Whether the sedentarisation of the nomadic pastoralist fitted in with the expansion of irrigated agriculture and whether any assimilation into new means of livelihood took place is also discussed.

Although the Aswan High Dam was constructed to promote the industrialisation and water security of Egypt it also resulted in the inundation of the region of Wadi Halfa and consequently the displacement of approximately 50,000 Sudanese Nubians. However, the Nubian resettlement and the sedentarisation of the pastoralist nomads to the New Halfa agricultural scheme can also be seen as an attempt by the Sudanese state to develop the agricultural sector, increase the utilisation of the River Atbara, to create employment and better living conditions for Sudanese people, and to increase the overall economic growth through export markets.

Understanding the various meanings behind the concept of development is important when looking at the cases of hydraulic and agricultural development in a country like Sudan. In recent history the world has seen many examples of large-scale hydraulic infrastructures being constructed and the mass population displacements and involuntary resettlement caused by them. Although it is generally agreed that hydraulic infrastructures such as dams do increase energy production and improve control over water flows, these development-induced mega-constructions tend to also cause severe environmental damage, population displacement and impoverishment (Cernea 1995). They depict development from a perspective of modernisation, growth and technological advancement with an emphasis on a top-down approach that is imposed upon the targeted people.

Therefore, it should be emphasised that people perceive development in subjective ways and development as an external force is hardly constructive. The construction of megaprojects such as dams tends to create inequitable socio-hydrological conditions, as the hydraulic infrastructures are often put forward by the people in political, economic and social power. This often leads to further unequal development, as the people without social power are often excluded from access to natural resources or the state of the resources deteriorates. Those in power also tend to justify their actions by laying claim to property rights and their exclusive rights to them (Swyngedouw 2009).

4.1 Displacement for development

Many top-down development initiatives include displacement and resettlement of people to make space for projects such as the construction of power plants, dams, mines and roads. This development-induced displacement (DID) is a form of population redistribution used by the government to develop environmental resource utilisation for the sake of benefiting the national economy (Grabska & Mehta 2008). It can also be seen as a tool for the government to implement changes in the existing political structure and as a form of social engineering. This is part of the larger agenda of the transformation of peripheral regions and under-populated areas into world economies (Plater 1994). Many problems emerge with displacement – such as drastic changes in livelihoods, loss of autonomy, indigenousness, traditions and established community networks. It is generally known that displacement causes disruption and loss of assets both within the community and for individuals and leads to a greater likelihood of impoverishment and reduced access to rights entitlement (Morvaridi 2008).

In many cases the displaced people have little or no say in deciding over the displacement, and although the projects usually have a plan for resettling the displaced people, it is mostly created without consulting the affected people. The displacement on its own is a heavy burden and many of the other negative consequences only emerge after the resettlement process. It is also important to shift from focusing on the needs of the displaced to a more rights based approach of displacement and resettlement. This includes active participation in the whole process of resettlement, rights to secure livelihoods, autonomy, land tenure rights and rights to self-sufficiency and citizenship (Grabska & Mehta 2008). In essence this comes down to acknowledging the rights of the displaced in deciding over their own lives and futures. As has been proven in many global instances, some displacement, even for the sake of development, may be inevitable. However the negative consequences of displacement could be mitigated or even avoided. This needs a thorough social impact assessment and the consultation of the people affected as well as a comprehensive resettlement plan.

4.2 Resettlement consequences

Many resettlement projects such as agricultural schemes are designed to benefit both the local displaced people and the country as a whole. In most cases the communities that face development-induced displacement are resettled into one of these schemes. Initially many resettlements were integrated into rural development plans, in order to improve the economic and social life of the rural poor in a way that would also contribute to the national economy (Barraclough et al. 1997). Particularly in North and East Africa large nomadic pastoral populations were incorporated into resettlement schemes as part of a sedentarisation campaign. Many nomadic groups are still seen as impediments to development and their support to the economy is seen as non-existant. Through the various objectives these resettlement projects have become instruments of nation building, economic growth and a means of promoting the nation's political profile (Plater 1994).

Since the 1950s the World Bank has been lending developing countries money for infrastructure projects and agricultural schemes in support of economic growth. Poverty alleviation has also been a core goal for the projects. Some of the expected outcomes of these projects were the modernisation and monetisation of rural society and a transition from traditional isolation to integration with the national and global economy (World Bank 1975). However, in many cases the resettlement schemes have proved to be failures. According to their own later evaluations on the rural development projects funded by the Bank, nearly half of the 262 projects have been deemed failures (World Bank 1989). Another study claims that only one of all the resettlement projects funded by the World Bank had involved adequate compensation and rehabilitation for those resettled. In all the other cases the displacements resulted in declining quality of life: nutrition, health, infant mortality, life expectancy and environmental sustainability (Nixon 2010). According to the records the economic performance of the resettlement schemes has also proved weak (Plater 1994).

Although many resettlement schemes do provide employment and services to those resettled, in many cases the long-term maintenance and monitoring plans are inadequate or non-existant. In essence the resettlement is not temporary, but should provide the resettled people and the forthcoming generations an opportunity to build a new life on a permanent basis. However the future scenarios are difficult to predict. The effect of global trends and changes in economy and agriculture has brought about unexpected impacts and the resettlement schemes have had to adapt to them. Many intangible factors such as social rootedness and lack of adaptability to new livelihoods and environments are tricky to evaluate and may only surface years later.

To be able to fight against these risks in the resettlement and reconstruction phase the nation should have strategies and the financial means to mitigate these negative consequences. However, in order for the resettlement to be successful and sustainable, one must also look at the factors of entitlement to rights, social articulation, integration and cultural well-being (Morvaridi 2008). As in the case of the Nubians in Egypt and Sudan, the resettlement caused an irreversible experience of social rejection from the government and bitterness about the lack of respect and protection for their traditional land, culture and livelihoods. Thus, the displacement and the resettlement that follows gives the impression that – for the nation – the utilisation of natural resources outweighs the integrity and continuity of its people's sustainable livelihoods and traditions.

An important factor to consider is also the extent to which resettlement affects the host population's future livelihoods. The resettlement of the Halfawi Nubians to New Halfa caused emerging inequalities between those that were to share the resources for the years to come – the resettled and the host population. The influx of other Sudanese into the scheme further changed the social composition. Therefore, resettlement projects should also consider the equal treatment and benefits of the host populations and ensure a more equal setting for the future sustainability of the scheme.

4.3 Land rights and territorialisation

People's access to land varies according to their social circumstances and the politics of land allocation. Whether decisions are made by traditional leaders, local or state government, or they are influenced by the actions of the global economy and privatisation policies; people's access to land varies greatly and can be highly unequal. The access to land, however, is socially determined and thus depends upon the social context people live in and who happens to have the power of decision-making (Eskonheimo 2006). Customarily, local traditional leaders have allocated lands to different communities or tribes, or people are accustomed to pastoralism and changing environments. In more recent history nation states have started to practice agricultural transformation, intensification and engineering – for instance in the form of agricultural irrigation schemes and the green revolution. People have gained access to land through property rights and land tenure systems (Eskonheimo 2006).

These changes have been particularly problematic when discussing the lifestyle of nomadic pastoralists. The land they have traditionally used for their pastoral needs is not owned by them, but rather is regarded as a common property resource (Eskonheimo 2006). In Sudan, as in many developing countries, the economic circumstances of nomadic pastoralists have deteriorated as a consequence of the government policies of favouring sedentary farming and the subsequent increased privatisation (Eskonheimo 2006). The land law of 1970 (Unregistered Land Act) left the Sudanese pastoralists and some subsistence farmers without rights to the lands they had traditionally used. Therefore it is clear to see that the Sudanese government has had a tendency to prioritise sedentary agriculture rather than nomadic agriculture (Eskonheimo 2006).

Many indigenous peoples or traditional communities do not have legal ownership or title deed to the environment they inhabit. They may have utilised the natural resources sustainably and lived in co-existence with nature, however without land ownership the land may not belong to them (Nixon 2010). Although territory has traditionally been connected with the political institution of the modern nation-state it is important to note that territories, large or small, are primarily social products and can range from national borders to homestead hedges and vague pastoral lands. It is basically an understanding of "inside and outside" or "secure and insecure". Seeing territories in social life, relationships and interactions depends therefore on the perspective (Delaney

2005). Thus, those with social, political or economic power define territories and territorialisation reflects and incorporates features of the social order that creates them (Delaney 2005; Minoia 2012). In the case of the construction of hydraulic dams many groups of people, who have traditionally inhabited the space that the planned hydraulic dam occupies, are forced to leave their socially determined territory. In most cases the final say in decision-making is within the nation-state that has the power to justify the social displacement, in the wake of the need to harness natural resources for the greater benefit.

Although territorial boundaries are mostly respected as a consequence of coercive force, the law and power, the boundaries can even aggravate social conflict and cause further resentment in those excluded (Delaney 2005). This is also the case with state or privatised territorialisation of natural resources which can cause social conflict, apathy towards the state and in some cases even exacerbate state disintegration. Unequal access to basic human needs such as water is also a problem that is related to territorialisation and power. The more recent question of the commodification of natural resources and, on the other hand, the growing demand for them is creating boundaries between those who have access to, say, clean drinking water and those who have not. Although water has its own spatial dynamic and resistance against attempts to channel its mobility (Natter & Zierhofer 2002), people, political entities and international actors are increasingly trying to privatise and commoditise it.

4.4 Social consequences of dams' construction and irrigation schemes

Mega-scale water projects have, for a long time, been included in development initiatives that aim to provide water and electricity for growing economies. Although many of the recently seen hydrological megaprojects have been essential in providing electricity for the growing urban needs around Africa and elsewhere in developing countries, they may have deepened the gap between those who have access to water resources, through economic or political power; and those who have been forced to step aside and utilise the resources left available for them. As stated in the Millennium Development Goals, provision of water and sanitation is a basic need and human right. However, it has also been stated that access to electricity and power is a prerequisite for the achievement of all Millennium Development Goals (Boege & Turner 2006). Therefore, although hydraulic engineering is providing electricity and enabling further national growth, it can also hinder development for some and make it impossible to continue practicing traditional livelihoods. The provision of electricity produced through dams rarely reaches the most rural communities. Hence, those people whose lives are directly altered due to the construction of large-scale water projects are forced to sacrifice and even face underdevelopment for the sake of larger good.

The growing need for water, energy and agricultural production is indisputable; however it is relevant to ask: Who has the power to decide over the physical changes in an area due to infrastructural engineering? Have the beneficiaries been openly identified and heard? Who on the other hand has to sacrifice their land and access to natural resources? The decisions over the changes in the biophysical conditions are often made by the socio-political elite in a country or a region, or – more recently – also by international organisations and multinational corporations. As water and other natural resources are becoming more and more commoditised it is often the less privileged or marginalised groups of people that suffer from these changes the most (Swyngedouw 2009; Minoia 2012). The political inequality in access to decision-making processes may also lead to unequal distribution of negative consequences and benefits from projects (Staddon 1988).

Often the communities directly affected by the infrastructural engineering are the ones who suffer the most and may even face issues of underdevelopment such as loss of cultural land and traditional means of income. Especially in a conflict-ridden country like Sudan, this is very alarming for the minority groups that are not well represented in national politics. The Nubian resettlement to New Halfa has by no means been the only social displacement in the history of Sudan. The recent Merowe Dam and Kajbar Dam constructions in the northern part of Sudan have led to protests and violent clashes with the local Nubians and government security forces as the Nubians are, again, threatened by the resettlement (International Rivers Network 2013).

It has also been argued that many agricultural schemes end up bringing more impoverishment and other negative consequences than development, and have consequently caused forced displacements of communities in various regions. The most affected people are usually subsistence farmers, herders, nomadic pastoralists and fishermen (Haydar 2008). These groups of people are often living on the periphery or are otherwise marginalised and therefore lack power when it comes to decision-making. For compensating the loss of their land, governments have resettled people in planned agricultural areas. This has been done cohesively with the planning of megaprojects such as dam constructions. The possibilities for irrigation and agricultural development have been portrayed as beneficial for the marginalised people thus lifting them out of previous poverty or otherwise traditional lifestyles. Many of these development initiatives have been carried out through assistance from international aid or investments (Haydar 2008). However, often the long-term consequences have not been thoroughly investigated and the negative impacts have not been properly assessed. The current state of many irrigation schemes needs further evaluation in order to plan new settlements more effectively and to understand the social consequences of hydroelectric projects and irrigation schemes.

Furthermore, the development of the irrigated agricultural sector may cause conflicts between nomadic pastoralists and farmers in irrigated agriculture. Conflict may arise between central governments, modern water sectors and the local communities over irrigation schemes and agricultural production for cash crops (Boege & Turner 2006). Negative impacts have been experienced in local communities that are highly dependent on subsistence economies and the local water resources. Those who have been forced to relocate due to development-induced displacement and resettlement have, in many instances, not benefited. On the contrary, many have become more impoverished by losing economic, social and cultural resources. Those who have been forcefully resettled due to the construction of water-related infrastructure often find themselves in conflict with the original people of the new resettlement area and the local government. Although national governments typically justify these development initiatives by invoking the larger goals of national growth and development it is often those already marginal who benefit the least and sacrifice the most for these initiatives (Haydar 2008).

Therefore, the economic, environmental and social consequences of hydraulic and agricultural development must be thoroughly examined prior to the development initiatives taking place, and the local communities affected should be allowed a strong say in decision-making and sharing of the benefits. Eventually this comes down to the question of to what extent can the ecosystem be modified for an intended development purpose and how, and between whom, the costs and benefits are shared. Hydropolitics will most likely become an even more critical issue within the countries sharing the Nile water basin. It is therefore crucial that the riparian countries maintain a good command of international policy and agreements as the actions of one riparian country may cause negative consequences to the entire downstream region.

5. The transforming sense of national identity in Sudan

When it comes to issues of land rights, territorialisation and social integration in Sudan the question of ethnicity and political power plays a key role. One of the underlying causes for the complexity of the national Sudanese identity is the variety and multitude of social and political hegemonies that have controlled and influenced the formation of Sudan today. The long history of conflict over power, resources and land has its roots in the different power hierarchies between ethnic groups that are based on the colonial foundation (Idris 2005). Prior to the independence of South Sudan in 2011, the population of the country as a whole was over 30 million people – consisting of over 570 heterogeneous ethnic and linguistic groups (Adar 2001; Collins 2008). Historically, these groups have been ruled by various political and ethnic establishments. The colonial construct together with the various eras of foreign rule have resulted in the ethnic and racial *community* becoming the basis for political and economic entitlement, instead of *citizenship*. The Sudanese government has failed to promote the development of a diverse yet equal society. This is often the reason for emerging tension and conflict as claims of marginalisation, exclusion and domination among the different ethnic groups are made (Idris 2005).

Since the British lost their control over the Sudan and independence was gained in 1956 the Sudanese government has pursued "ethno-religious-centred policies" of Islamisation and Arabisation throughout the country (Adar 2001; Collins 2008). In essence Arabisation means integrating other ethnic or religious groups into the "cultural values and beliefs of Muslims and Arabs in particular" (Adar 2001). This Islamisation has resulted in the polarisation of the country into cultural core-peripheries and also further exacerbated the crisis of Darfur and the secession of South Sudan in 2011. The ruling elite in Sudan has long seen the ethnic diversity as an obstacle and a disintegrating factor in the unification of Sudan. Adopting the Arab-Islamic paradigm was therefore used to ensure national unity (Biong Deng 2005). This however has divided the nation, created a power imbalance between different ethnic groups and deepened the gap between the core and the peripheries. Many of the crises in Sudan's history have been caused by the exclusionary and discriminatory policies adopted by the ruling elite against the majority of the indigenous people – policies that have denied their access to political and social decision-making, and therefore, often to power and resources (Biong Deng 2005; Idris 2005).

However, as we have seen with the secession of South Sudan and the possibility of the secession of Darfur and other peripheral regions of Sudan, the country is witnessing vast disparities and extensive differentiation regarding accessibility, wealth and societal status when it comes to the different ethnic groups of Sudan. The politics of Arabisation and the cultural mainstreaming create automatic hierarchies, inclusion and exclusion, that with a country as big as Sudan, means there are bound to be conflicts and power struggles between different groups of people. As with many African countries, Sudan has also been an artificial construct combining many geographically, religiously and ethnically different regions (Cockett 2010).

One of the negative consequences of this cultural mainstreaming is the decaying of the multitude of cultures, traditions and historical symbols within the country. For instance, the lack of interest regarding the rich archaeological findings of old Nubia – many of which are now under Lake Aswan. This imposed single vision of history and the Sudanese identity has neglected or destroyed the presence of a rich cultural and historical capital within Sudan. As Amir Idris states; "In the Sudanese context, history has never been about the past, but about the present contested realities." (Idris 2005).

5.1 The Nubians of Wadi Halfa

"Nubia is a detached country, and the Nubians remained tied to their region, living in a world of their own." (Hassan Dafalla 1975)

The relative isolation of the region of Nubia in the north of Sudan and south of Egypt had led to the creation of a distinct and unique Nubian culture. Nubia used to be topographically, historically and ethnically a single country that was later divided by the arbitrary border of Egypt and Sudan. After the decline of ancient Egypt, Nubia remained an independent area until the Arabs came to Sudan and brought the influence of Islam with them (Dafalla 1975). The Nubians belong to the Hamitic group of Africa and the long formation of their identity has been much discussed. Hassan Dafalla describes the Nubians as peaceful yet demanding and strong advocates of their rights (Dafalla 1975).

Despite their relatively high level of education, rich cultural history and distinct culture, the Nubians have, for a long time, been discriminated against within both Egypt and Sudan. Many of the particular cultural traits and characteristics of the Nubians have evolved over a long period of time in their distinct environment in Wadi Halfa and its surroundings. I will look at some of the characteristics of the Nubians in order to better understand the difficulties of adapting to the different environment of New Halfa.

Besides farming, the date palm formed the backbone of the Nubian economy. It was the symbol of wealth and also a concrete sign of security for future generations. At certain places along the Nile the riverbanks were covered with a high date palm forest (Dafalla 1975). Apart from income and security the palms gave shelter from the desert sun and were the source of inspiration for poetry and singing, to an almost sacred extent. It is known as one of the symbols of Nubian culture and besides being a source of livelihood and food, the palm leaves had an important meaning in many cultural ceremonies (Dafalla 1975). All the date palms were later inundated by water when the Aswan High Dam slowly pooled the area into a lake. The Nubians, however, were already relocated and thus saved from the sight. Back in their new home of New Halfa the date palm does not seem to thrive and only a few are grown, mostly for aesthetic and symbolic reasons. They are not kept for economic gain anymore but as a constant reminder of the old way of life and the cultural roots that lie deep, somewhere else than in the flat clay soils of the Butana plain.

Besides sparse rainfall, the Nile was the only source of irrigation in Wadi Halfa. Traditional waterwheels, *Sagiyas*, were used for irrigation. Agricultural methods were not modern and the plots were relatively small. A rich variety of vegetables and fruit were grown according to the winter and summer rotation and the flood plain cultivation. An interesting aspect of the Nubian lifestyle in Wadi Halfa was the emigration of the working-age men to work in urban regions while the women stayed behind looking after the orchards. In a census carried out prior to the displacement of the Nubians they discovered that nearly every cultivator in a tenancy was female (Dafalla 1975). Due to the migration for work of the working-age men, a lot of the plots were given to caretakers or closest kin to utilise (Dafalla 1975). Nubians were thus already accustomed to absentees in farming in Wadi Halfa, and farmlands were often shared among larger families.

The Nubian language is a strong continuation of the culture that is still used in New Halfa. However, many turn to Arabic in public discussions, thus making the Nubians also more adapted to the Arab culture and language (Dafalla 1975; Adar 2001). Despite this the Nubian language continues to have a great meaning for many. The seclusion of the Nubians is also visible in the tendency to cling together instead of mixing with other communities. Marriage takes place within the Nubian boundaries and traditional ceremonies are present in all turning points of social life. The Nubian women wore traditionally long black dresses made of thin lace that protected them from the sun yet allowed a cooling breeze to pass through in the arid desert climate of Wadi Halfa. In New Halfa the tradition was not as prevalent, as the clay soil became muddy when wet and consequently made the dresses dirty. The distinct Nubian architecture of bold patterns on the walls and other decorations that were common in typical Nubian houses in Wadi Halfa are no longer continued in New Halfa (Haydar 2008). It is probable that the government-built houses in New Halfa felt alien and too impersonal to suit the decorations.

The traditional Nubian lifestyle could not be fully sustained in the different environment of the Butana region in Eastern Sudan and some cultural aspects have been abandoned. The Nubians of Wadi Halfa had to sacrifice greatly for the greater development of the country, but also for their own future survival.

The stable lifestyle on their ancestral land turned into a challenging lifestyle as a tenant farmer with shifting crop prices and other insecurities. Besides the undeniable losses of tradition and cultural traits, the resettlement came as an insult to their dignity. Unable to protest the changes many Nubian characteristics and cultural customs were slowly merged into the mainstream Sudanese culture (Dafalla 1975). Evidently this is true within the Nubians of New Halfa today. However, according to the interviews conducted for this study it appears that the Nubian identity and consciousness is resistant to change. Even if their cultural traditions and customs have lost some of their distinctiveness they continue to safeguard their self-worth.

However, it is important to remember that even before the building of the Aswan High Dam the ancient Nubian lifestyle was bound to change sooner or later. Before the construction of the first Aswan dam the Nubians had to leave their farms to work in towns such as Cairo, Alexandria and Khartoum. The land of old Nubia may have high cultural value but in terms of arable land it was not enough to support the growing population (Haydar 2008). Therefore the traditional lifestyle was subject to modernisation and the Nubians were already actively changing it. However, it may be that the feeling of loss and nostalgia that Nubians continue to feel until this day is not so much about the concrete loss of their land but about the discrimination and insult they experienced with the inundation of Wadi Halfa, the loss of cultural integrity and the lack of ownership in deciding their future course.

5.2 Sacrifices of land and identity

The building of the Aswan High Dam and the resettlement of approximately 50,000 Sudanese Nubians in 1963 (Dafalla 1975) to New Halfa also fit together with the direction of Sudanese nationalism as it destroyed the old town of Wadi Halfa and many traditional cultural lands of ancient Nubia in Northern Sudan. The New Halfa agricultural scheme was built in order to resettle the Nubians from the north and to sedentarise many nomadic groups of Eastern Sudan, in order to make them to join the agricultural scheme. This was supposed to make it easier for these formerly self-sufficient and isolated groups to be absorbed into the Sudanese nation as well as to promote the growing economy of Sudan (Jok 2007). The Sudanese government's exclusionary policies were not just based on religious differences, but the post-colonial policies attempted to eradicate the indigenous traditions and cultures of the non-Arab populations within the north (Jok 2007).

The question of whether the Nubian people of Wadi Halfa were intentionally resettled and integrated to the Sudanese and Egyptian societies and economies is relevant and still widely discussed within the Nubian communities. Although resettled Nubians were compensated with money, land and housing, when it comes to losses of heritage, culture and traditions it is difficult to compensate such aspects of life. Although the construction of the Aswan High Dam – for the supply of power and agricultural irrigation – was the main cause for the destruction of old Nubia in Wadi Halfa and the resettlement of its people, some scholars have argued that it was a part of the *demographic engineering* of Sudan that is still taking place (Hashim 2010).

Sudanese academic Jalal Hashim argues that the continuing construction of dams in Northern Sudan is a way to create irrigated agricultural land for Egyptian farmers and, at the same time, break-up the existing Nubian communities in the area and incorporate them into the Sudanese society (Hashim 2010). The old land of Nubia was for a long time a distinct cultural territory – something that was in the interest of both Egypt and Sudan to divide and disperse. Breaking the territorial hegemony of the Nubians made it easier for the governments to gain control over these areas and impose Sudanese and Egyptian nationalism. In essence it was about replacing the territories of ethnic identity with political territories controlled by the central government. Adherance and opposition to Sudanese politics largely defined the territorial areas of core and periphery. These experiences of unequal distribution of land and the regulation of customary rights to land are felt by many different Sudanese ethnic communities, the Darfur conflict being just one example.

It is debatable to what extent ethnic policies played a role in the Aswan High Dam planning process. Practically, however, it must also be stressed that the location of the construction of dams is only possible in the places where the cataracts are located and are thus defined by natural factors such as topography and hydrology.

6. Study Area: the New Halfa Agricultural Scheme

The New Halfa agricultural scheme started as the largest known planned resettlement project in Sudan at the time, as a consequence of the construction of the Aswan High dam that caused the inundation of the historical town of Wadi Halfa under Lake Nasser (Ahmad & Abu Sin 1990; Laxen 2007). The New Halfa scheme was partly funded by Egypt as compensation, as it was important for Egypt to secure the construction of the Aswan High Dam (Laxen 2007). Out of six alternative sites for the relocation of the Nubians, the location of Khasm el Girba was eventually selected, as the Khasm el Girba dam was completed in 1964 to support irrigated agriculture (NHAPC 2011). The project was established between 1964 and 1969 and in 1964 the transfer of the majority of the Nubians took place (Dafalla 1975; Sørbø 1985).

The New Halfa scheme had many objectives: 1) It was to resettle about 50,000 Halfawi from the old Wadi Halfa 2) it was to settle the nomadic tribes that used to enjoy grazing and cultivation rights prior to the project and provide them with social services, better economic conditions and agriculture opportunities; 3) it was to increase national income and foreign exchange earnings by growing cotton and groundnuts; 4) to promote self-sufficiency in wheat and sugar cane; 5) to utilise Atbara River waters more efficiently 5) and to utilise the fertile area of the so-called "Butana region", a grazing land formerly used by nomadic tribes for livestock grazing (Abdelrazig 1979; Haydar 2008; NHAPC 2011).

The New Halfa Agricultural Scheme is an agricultural settlement scheme of 440,000 feddans in size. The area of New Halfa is situated about 400 km east of Khartoum, in the western part of Kassala State (Laxen 2007). The scheme lies on the Butana plain and is located in the catchment area of the Atbara River. At the time of the establishment of the New Halfa Scheme it was the second largest irrigation project in the Sudan after the Gezira Scheme, still the largest irrigation scheme in the world (Sørbø 1985).

The water coming through the Khasm el Girba dam in the Atbara River is managed by the irrigation department of Sudan (NHAPC 2011). The irrigation system is based on gravity flow, where the main canal conveys water to the project area through the network of subsidiary canals together with the help of motorised pumps (Laxen 2007, Haydar 2008). The irrigation network consists of branch canals, major and minor canals, quaternary canals and tertiary farm ditches. The traditional method of the basin (Angaya) system is used in field irrigation (NHAPC 2011). Despite the canal system, there are great water losses due to evaporation which decreases water availability (Haydar 2008). The Khasm el Girba dam was completed in 1964. It can supply water to the main canal by different methods of operation depending on the difference in the water levels between the reservoir and the canal (NHAPC 2011). The dam was originally designed to hold 1.3 billion cubic metres of water; however, by 1976 the storage capacity of the reservoir was reduced to 0.8 billion cubic metres due to heavy siltation coming from the upper reaches of the river Atbara in the Ethiopian highlands (Laxen 2007). At the moment the capacity of the reservoir is approximately 0.6 billion (Taha 2010; NHAPC 2011). During the growing season the water usually flows continuously to the minor canals. However, some farmers have complained that certain areas get more water than others. Due to the declining capacity of the reservoir the irrigation area is consequently decreasing.

Each agricultural settler received a *hawasha* (tenancy) of 15 feddans to grow cotton, wheat or sorghum and groundnuts. Cotton was chosen as it is the major cash crop for generating hard currency for the government and profit for the tenants. Groundnuts are the second most important cash crop in the scheme and wheat and sorghum were cultivated for local consumption and the surplus was sold (Ahmed 2009). The Nubians from Wadi Halfa also received freehold land as compensation for their lost land in Northern Sudan (El Arifi 1988). Originally there were 22,367 tenants in the scheme, however later it was noticed that not all tenants reside in the project area. From the start the absentee rate was already 40 % (Abdelrazig 1979).

The New Halfa scheme was originally a joint venture between the government and the tenants. The tenant provides the labour and supervision while the government provides the irrigation facilities, scheme administration, agricultural services, transportation and marketing of cotton (Abdelrazig 1979). The New Halfa Agricultural Production Corporation (NHAPC) is the central body responsible for the management of the scheme within the framework of the objectives set out in the original plan. NHAPC was also designated to provide technical assistance and agricultural services for the farmers. It is also responsible for choosing where and which crops will be cultivated, the timing and ensuring the execution of the various agricultural operations, for providing water, fertiliser, pesticides as well as for setting the policy for pricing and for the allocation of tenancies, credits and field supervision (Haydar 2008). The New Halfa Agricultural Corporation was to initiate agricultural reform in the project area in order to maximise social and economic benefits. In accordance with the agreement between the tenant and the Corporation, the share cropping applies only to cotton and the wheat/sorghum and groundnuts belong to the tenant who pays the Corporation for the services it provides (Abdelrazig 1979).

However, since the start of the scheme, problems have started to emerge. In 1977 Abdelrazig had already pointed out problems in the Khasm el Girba Dam, such as a shortage of water caused by increased sedimentation and blockage by weeds, defective farm and canal layouts and inefficient application of irrigation water by tenants. In addition a shortage of fuels and increasing fertiliser and insecticide prices were experienced (Abdelrazig 1979). Later on, the total cultivable land was reduced and the storage capacity of the Khasm el Girba dam is now reduced to 0.6 million cubic metres (NHAPC 2011).

6.1 The town of New Halfa and the surrounding villages

New Halfa town is the administrative and commercial centre and it is situated at the centre of the scheme (Ahmad & Abu Sin 1990). Although a largely residential area, it is the commercial and trade centre of the scheme with numerous private businesses, informal markets and public services such as the hospital. The town of New Halfa has developed extensively since the start of the scheme. It is still surrounded by mainly Nubian and Shukriya villages. Other ethnic groups, such as nomadic groups, are located in the peripheral regions further away from the town. Consequently access to services varies greatly between the different residents within the scheme, depending upon their location. Due to the population increase the town is supposed to be providing urban amenities to approximately ten times the original population of New Halfa and it is struggling to meet the growing demand for public services (Ahmad & Abu Sin 1990). During the 1993 census the population in the whole scheme area was already 385,250 which has since increased due to natural growth (NHAPC 2011).

The growth of migrant labour and urbanisation has generated many informal businesses that are scattered throughout the town. This influx of people has also resulted in the growing amount of squatters and settlements emerging near the town that are not officially recognised by the scheme. The competition over free land has caused some land disputes between the original inhabitants, internal refugees and migrants, merchants and the Shukriya tenants who are claiming rights to some of the vacant land in the town (Ahmad & Abu Sin 1990). The pressure within the town is understandable as the services available were initially designed to meet the needs of the original residents, not the tenfold population of today.

Most of the surrounding villages in close proximity to the town were built at the time of the construction of the scheme and allocated to both Halfawi Nubians and to local ethnic groups such as Shukriya, Hadendowa and Rashaida, among others. The Halfawi villages are all situated close to the town, but most of the villages of the indigenous ex-nomadic or semi-nomadic tribes are further away and built to a much lower standard than the Nubian villages (Ahmad & Abu Sin 1990). Some of the nomads have also constructed their own houses in contrast to the Nubians who were all given houses by the scheme (Sørbø 1977). Villages designated for the nomads have also less extensive social services and amenities (Sørbø 1977; Haydar 2008). The communities are segregated and dispersed with agricultural land acting as buffer zones (Haydar 2008). Interestingly, as far back as 1975 the manager of the Scheme, Osman Idris, claimed that the inequalities between the social services in the villages have "slowed down any progress and paralysed any interest in agriculture" (Sørbø 1977). Therefore, social inequalities were rooted in the scheme from the start.

The 50,000 Nubians originally resettled were placed in either pre-built brick houses constructed in 25 villages in the scheme area, or in the town of New Halfa itself (Laxen 2007). The Nubian villages consist of about 300 families and communities resettled according to their former home villages in Wadi Halfa. Of all the tenancies approximately one third was given to members of the local population which had inhabited the region as semi-nomadic pastoralists. Besides the 15 feddans of land, each of the Nubian tenants also received some freehold land for vegetable growing and subsistence farming depending on their loss of land in the now inundated Wadi Halfa (Laxen 2007). The compensation was justified, however it created inequalities between the Halfawi Nubians and the local host populations who were compensated less.

The construction of the Khasm el Girba dam and the New Halfa scheme demanded a workforce that arrived from other parts of Sudan, mainly from West and Central Sudan. Many of these remained in the scheme as farm workers and lived in informal settlements scattered within the scheme. Some of these settlements became permanent but most of them still remain unofficial and are not recognised by the scheme. The inhabitants of the informal settlements have been generally divided between the landless and the so-called Arabs, of which the landless are mainly from Western Sudan and the Arabs from Eastern Sudan (Laxen 2007).

The deteriorating state of the infrastructure is causing problems for the scheme residents and the poor maintenance of tarmacked roads or lack thereof is a challenge for transportation, especially during the rainy season when the soils become muddy. The number of farm workers, internally displaced people from conflict areas and foreign refugees, has also increased in New Halfa causing further demand for services and housing (Ahmad & Abu Sin 1990). For instance, the town of New Halfa has only one hospital and therefore struggles to provide some basic health care services to the population of New Halfa and the growing settlements surrounding it. In 1990 the hospital of New Halfa – with less than 300 beds – was already having to provide services for half a million inhabitants of the scheme. This has been a challenge, as the scheme has encountered serious outbreaks of waterborne diseases especially bilharzia, malaria and leishmaniasis that are diseases endemic to the area (Ahmad & Abu Sin 1990; Laxen 2007).

6.2 The ethnic composition of New Halfa today

Traditionally the area of New Halfa was inhabited by various nomadic ethnic groups; particularly the indigenous pastoral Shukriya (Haydar 2008, NHAPC 2011). However, when the Khasm el Girba dam and the New Halfa scheme were constructed they profoundly changed not only the physical, but also the ethnic landscape of the area. Generally the ethnic composition can be divided into tenant farmers, mostly of Nubian origin (the resettled Halfawi Nubians) (30 %), the traditional Butana nomadic groups of Shukriya, Beja and Rashaida tribes (60 %) and the Western and the Eastern Sudanese landless people and the migrant workers (10 %) (Laxen 2007; Haydar 2008). It is important to note that the Halfawi Nubians comprise only approximately 30 % of the total population in the scheme even though the scheme was originally established primarily

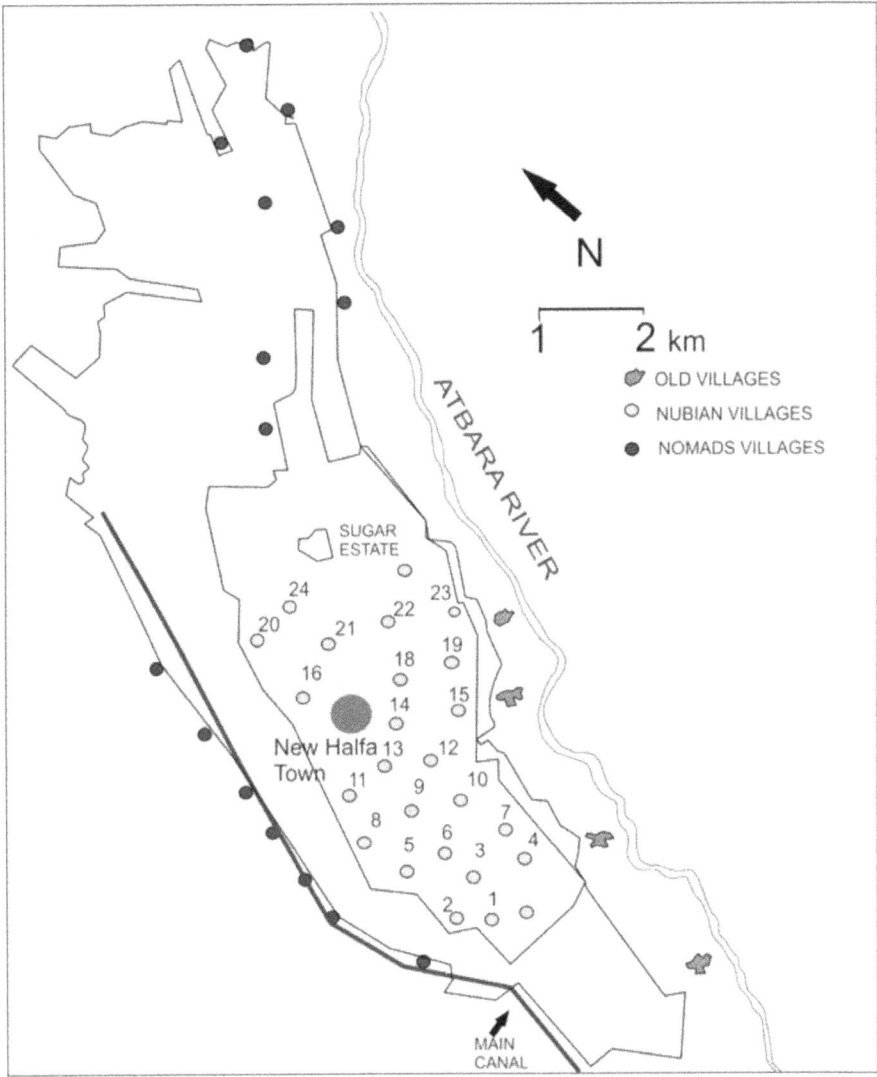

Figure 2. New Halfa agricultural scheme and the settlements. The mostly Nubian villages are officially named by numbers. The map shows that the Nubians were located in the central part of the scheme whereas the nomadic and semi-nomadic groups were further away.

to resettle the Halfawis. The Shukriya are the dominant tribe in the area, but there are also smaller tribes such as the Arabic-speaking Lahawyien, Ahamda, Kawahla, Khawalda and Rashaida as well as the Beja-speaking Hadendowa, Beni Amer, Amrar and Bisharien. The nomadic tribes were also settled in the scheme, mostly on the outskirts, and the government hoped to sedentarise them for purposes of better revenue and state control (See figure 2.) (Haydar 2008).

Most of the Western and Eastern Sudanese landless people are migrant labourers from Fur, Zaghawa and Tama tribes originating from western parts of Sudan and some pastoral groups from the eastern parts of Sudan such as Beni Amer and Hadendowa (Laxen 2007). In addition the area has smaller populations of labourers that originally came from the Nuba Mountains in Central Sudan and of West African origin and increasingly former refugees from Eritrea (Sørbø 1985; Laxen 2007). Most of the Western and South-Western Sudanese immigrants had already arrived in New Halfa between the 1960s and 1980s during the drought in western parts of Sudan. The poorest of the landless immigrant population is settled in the outskirt camps of the scheme (Laxen 2007).

The ethnic composition within New Halfa and its surroundings is difficult to divide into groups, and there are different ways of differentiating between landless and nomadic groups according to the various sources. However, for this study it is important to differentiate between the Nubians from Wadi Halfa, the nomadic groups of the original area of New Halfa scheme that were partly incorporated into the scheme economy, and the landless migrant groups, such as internally displaced people (IDPs), that have joined new Halfa from various regions throughout Sudan. Many of these landless migrant groups tend to practice different livelihoods from waged farm labour to small businesses and transportation with donkey carts (Laxen 2007).

The nomadic groups such as Shukriya, Rashaida and the Beja-speaking groups such as Hadendowa are integrated to the scheme to a varying extent. Some of the Shukriya groups were able to benefit from the scheme and become farmers whereas some did not. The Rashaida originally emigrated from Saudi Arabia some 150 years ago and mostly engage with farming and camel herding practices. They tend to be isolated within the scheme and keep contact with Saudi Arabia in the form of remittances (Laxen 2007). The other Beja-speaking groups also continue with pastoralism and engage in farming and other activities in the scheme to different extents but also feel like outsiders within the scheme (Laxen 2007).

Although the Nubians resisted the resettlement and relocation to New Halfa, many migrant labourers chose to relocate there in hope of finding employment in the agricultural sector. It is therefore noteworthy that many of the people working on farms or in the informal sector originate from other parts of Sudan or are internally displaced people that have had to flee the on-going conflicts in

Western Sudan, such as in Darfur, the Nuba Mountains and the region that is now South Sudan. Sudan has more than five million internally displaced people making it the highest producer of IDPs in the world (Assal 2008). The internal armed conflicts throughout Sudan have caused massive population displacements and many have settled in the regions within Eastern Sudan. Many have come to New Halfa by choice in search of better employment opportunities and living conditions. Some have also been resettled due to the government's experiment of relocating the IDPs to the productive areas, such as mechanised agricultural schemes like New Halfa, in order to promote their self-reliance (Assal 2008).

The New Halfa scheme is also home to many former Eritrean refugees, who have decided to stay within the scheme. The economic opportunities are better within Sudan and the irrigation schemes, such as New Halfa, provide seasonal employment opportunities for many Eritreans in East Sudan. For them it has been easy to assimilate into the region as many ethnic origins and cultural and religious practices, are shared. For example the Beni Amer in East Sudan have the same ethnic roots as some Eritreans (Kibreab 2008). Many of the Sudanese IDPs and the former Eritrean refugees have found the irrigation schemes provide opportunities that prevent them from going back to their original homes. However, in contrast to people displaced by development, such as the Halfawi Nubians in New Halfa, the IDPs and refugees that fled conflict areas have not been compensated and many of them lack the opportunities to exercise rights in their host areas (Assal 2008). In the case of New Halfa, these groups of people are often treated as secondary citizens, and their rights are being disregarded. Although they have provided the scheme with an important workforce for a long period of time, many of them continue to have an unrecognised status, remain neglected and have therefore limited and unequal access to services and agricultural opportunities within the scheme.

Therefore, the Nubians that used to inhabit a very secluded and ethnically homogeneous area in the north of Sudan are now living in a multi-ethnic environment of nomadic tribes and agricultural workers from all around Sudan (Sørbø 1977; Ahmad & Abu Sin 1990). However, it was not just the Nubians but all the new residents of the agricultural scheme that had to adjust to a physically and culturally different environment and the new lifestyle required by the tenancy farming system. The Nubians have expressed some concern over the changing ethnic landscape of the scheme, as the influx of now sedentary nomads and agricultural workers continues to grow. The Nubians initially agreed to resettle in New Halfa thinking it would be a "closed" area where they could maintain their identity and continuity of their cultural traditions (Ahmad & Abu Sin 1990). Before resettling to New Halfa, the Nubians in Wadi Halfa had very limited knowledge of the rest of the Sudan and some considered themselves more Egyptian than Sudanese (Dafalla 1975). Therefore, the adjustment to the new environment of New Halfa may have caused the Halfawi to further isolate themselves from the rest of the inhabitants of the scheme in order to preserve their cultural customs and lifestyles.

In more recent years, due to a population influx from elsewhere in Sudan, the Nubians have also become an ethnic minority in New Halfa, which has possibly further hindered their motivation for integrating into the multi-ethnic environment of New Halfa. Since then, many Nubians have become more urbanised and have left New Halfa to settle in the suburbs of Khartoum where one may find a community of many Nubians originating from Wadi Halfa. However, despite the multicultural composition of the scheme residents, the ethnic groups continue to remain within their own social compounds and lack of equal social interaction remains. During the resettlement process the different ethnic groups were settled separately due to their different origins and customs (World Bank 1992). As a result the scheme is socially fragmented and lacks affinity.

6.3 Changes and challenges in New Halfa

The New Halfa agricultural scheme of today is quite different from the original plan set out for it in the early 1960s. The original objectives and expectations have not been fully met and the scheme has caused various disappointments to both the government and the tenants. The long-term production plans of the corporation were based on the assumption that the cropped land would remain constant and each tenant would continue growing the three crops annually in rotation. However, due to the scarcity of irrigation water the targeted cropping intensity was never reached. This reduced the irrigated farm land and consequently deteriorated the living standards and economic situation of many tenants (Ahmed 2009). Due to this many tenants had to look for various additional sources of income, some accumulated extra tenancies and some abandoned the scheme altogether.

The deterioration of the scheme started in the 1970s and has been further aggravated ever since. From the beginning the water canals became sedimented and the land fertility decreased. The yields were lower than expected causing further challenges for the farmer. The underlying cause of the poor performance is the reduced amount of water in the Khasm el Girba Dam due to the siltation of alluvial deposits from the Atbara River (Sørbø 1977). In addition, the rainfall is highly variable and weeds have increasingly started to infest the canals. The invasive species of Mesquite (Prosopis juliflora) invaded 40 % of agricultural land in New Halfa and blocked water canals but it was later eradicated by the Sudanese government (Laxen 2007). The vehicle pool provided by the New Halfa Agricultural Corporation has also deteriorated as much equipment has broken down and spares have not been imported (Sørbø 1977; Sørbø 1985). According to the interviews conducted for this study this was still the case in 2011. Many respondents complained about the lack of machinery and having to rely on manual labour instead.

For the Nubians the conditions proved disappointing and resulted in lack of attachement to their new home. As a consequence some left the scheme and moved to the suburbs of Khartoum in search of a more urban career. Some continued farming in New Halfa in the form of absentee landlordism while pursuing other professions. In addition to this the increasing urbanisation and the growing employment opportunities in Khartoum made life in New Halfa seem less appealing, especially for the younger generation. Consequently, those with the financial possibility to relocate to Khartoum left New Halfa together with their capital and assets, thus leaving behind the poor and the persevering (Haydar 2008).

There were also many push factors for Halfawi leaving New Halfa and moving to suburban Khartoum. Issues identified were difficulties in cultivation such as a shortage of irrigation water, numerous fees and rising input costs, contaminated drinking water, deteriorating or collapsed social services, unemployment, diseases such as malaria and bilharzia and deteriorating crop prices. Many of the houses built by the government also turned out to have asbestos roofs that caused health problems such as asthma and cancer. On the other hand, urban Khartoum proved to have better employment opportunities, social services and less waterborne diseases. The Nubians also found it easy to blend in with the already existing Halfawi communities in the suburbs of Khartoum (Haydar 2008). The growing tenant absenteeism has therefore been a serious challenge to the scheme since the start. An explanation for the high rate of absentees was presented by Sørbø when he stated that the resettled Nubians received tenancies in the scheme despite their original occupations and previous means of livelihood in Wadi Halfa. This meant that they tended to hire farm workers to cultivate their land while pursuing other occupations elsewhere. Secondly, the income from cultivation proved unstable and inadequate. Many Nubians chose to hand over their given tenancies to a relative who then acted on their behalf while the other pursued their careers elsewhere. Therefore, tenant absenteeism and tenancy accumulation have existed in the scheme since the start and are still taking place today (Sørbø 1977; Haydar 2008). This has resulted in increasing differentiation among tenants as others have become more competitive in agricultural production compared to the tenants with fewer tenancies to cultivate.

It has been argued that the challenges faced in New Halfa have further deepened the class differentiation, as the wealthier tenants were able to give credit to poorer tenants, thus enabling the scheme to operate even though the poorer tenants did not receive enough income from cultivation to survive but – in addition – had to take out credit (Sørbø 1985). As a consequence the gap between the richer and the poorer started to widen. This was further aggravated by the fact that, right from the start of the scheme, people were separated according to ethnic background, which led to growing differentiation between villages. The Nubians received houses in central locations as compensation but most of the nomads and migrants had to construct their own houses on the outskirts. Due to this the living conditions vary greatly within the scheme. The services do not reach to all villages and many villages of nomads and migrants are excluded from the infrastructure network. However, the Halfawi villages are well connected to the infrastructure with electricity, piped water and services compared to the other villages.

It is important to remember, however, that the situation in New Halfa cannot be evaluated in isolation from the negative socio-economic and political conditions that have taken place in Sudan (Haydar 2008). The yields have been low and below targets due to the overall environmental degradation and periods of drought seen in the region. At the same time the production costs have risen and the profitability of cash crops has fluctuated. The impact of political and social conflict and overall development challenges have also been experienced in New Halfa.

6.4 Social consequences of the resettlement of the Halfawi Nubians

The Sudanese President Abboud addressed the Nubian people on December 6th 1959, before the resettlement and the inundation of Wadi Halfa, by stating: *"I promise to accept your choice of place, wherever you want to go, in any part of the Sudan, and that none of you will be forced to go anywhere against his will."* However, although the people of Wadi Halfa were able to vote on various locations identified for possible resettlement, and the vast majority of votes went for Kadaru area and the north Gezira Extension South of Khartoum, the location of Khasm el Girba was eventually chosen by the government, against the will of the majority of people who were to be resettled there (Dafalla 1975). Although the government tried to reassure the Halfawi in Wadi Halfa of the benefits of Khasm el Girba as a location by ensuring freehold land, developed infrastructure and other benefits, the Halfawi were more afraid of resettling into a completely different environment from Wadi Halfa (Dafalla 1975). The government addressed the Halfa people and spoke with admiration of the great sacrifice they made for the benefit of their homeland (Dafalla 1975).

The government had built numerous villages for Halfawi in New Halfa with housing, services and cultivable land. They assured the people that the land was fertile, it was not a heavily populated area and all the villages would be joined together by a road system. The area would also have a railway link with Khartoum, Kassala and Port Sudan. Although it was known that the area had some endemic diseases such as Bilharzia it was said that adequate medical services would be provided (Dafalla 1975). This was indeed the case at the beginning of the scheme and the people, at least the Halfawi, were provided with adequate services.

When the Halfawi arrived by trains from Wadi Halfa, their life seemed very different from what it used to be and they had to adapt to a different climate, environment and various ethnic groups compared to the relative isolation of Wadi Halfa. The new way of cultivation on broad new *hawashas* took time to adapt to and many of the staple foods grown in Wadi Halfa could not be grown in New Halfa (Dafalla 1975). In later years, many Nubians grew accustomed to New Halfa, but continued to sentimentally regard Wadi Halfa as their ancestral home.

It has also been argued that the resettlement of the Nubians, both in Sudan and Egypt, to new areas was part of the cultural assimilation into the dominant Sudanese and Egyptian culture and economy (Haydar 2008). For many cultural and ethnic groups this is a natural consequence of state nationalism that has taken place throughout the world, but the difference in forced resettlements is that it often happens very rapidly without the necessary time for adjustment and unprompted assimilation. Although the reasons behind the resettlement of the Halfawi Nubians is already known at this stage, there is little agreement as to why the resettlement schemes often end up a disappointment for both the government and the people. The benefits of the dam, however, are high enough to justify the resettlement. Besides the compensation, the actual social costs of resettlement are rarely calculated (Haydar 2008).

6.5 Sedentarisation of pastoral nomads in New Halfa region

The Butana grazing lands of the region have long been migrated by the nomadic pastoralist groups such as the Beja tribes of Hadendowa and the Shukriya tribes. Moving around the region according to changing seasons in search of water and grazing land, this ancient lifestyle has remained resilient to change. The importance of pastoralism as a livelihood system in this arid region has proved environmentally and socially sustainable. The various ways they have adapted to the environment and have developed their livelihoods according to the resources available, within time and place, should be regarded as a highly developed symbiotic relationship with the surrounding land.

However, in many cases the pastoralists have been seen as backward and opposed to modernisation and development. Their contribution to food production is often ignored and their pastoral livelihood is seen as detrimental to the environment. With times of increasing demand for efficient land use and reform of land tenure, the pastoral lifestyle has been seen as out of control and out of reach by the state (Ahmed 2001). It has therefore been the objective to sedentarise the nomadic population. Since the increase in mechanised agriculture the grazing lands have slowly diminished, and the access to water has become more challenged. Many nomadic groups have had to adapt to the decreasing land availability and to consider agricultural activities as an alternative livelihood. However, as Abdel Ahmed argues, the externally oriented and dependent development model of unequal exchange relations does not offer a favourable alternative to the existing nomadic livelihood (Ahmed 2002). The change from an independent and flexible lifestyle to state controlled agricultural production is drastic and the exclusion of nomadic pastoralists in the planning process may cause resistance within the nomadic groups.

With the construction of agricultural irrigation schemes such as New Halfa the pastoralists were initially compensated for the reduction in grazing land. Many received free access to agricultural residues in the schemes or they were incorporated into the scheme as resident farmers (Sørbø 1985; Shazali & Ahmed 1999). However, as the pastoral lands were not legally registered to the pastoral nomads prior to the scheme, the compensation agreements were detrimental to the pastoralists. Compared to the Nubians the nomads received less provision of services and housing (Sørbø 1985). It has also been stated that the pastoralists have been politically marginalised and thus unable to defend or understand their rights (Shazali & Ahmed 1999). Although many services, such as education and health care, were made available to the nomadic groups because of the scheme, it is not clear whether this has prevented them from being further marginalised.

When the construction of the New Halfa agricultural scheme started, the local Shukriya of the Butana region were not pleased about the expropriation of their land. They asked for compensation for the loss of their land and an agreement was made to pay the Shukriya Arabs and other local ethnic groups and to give them tenancy grants distinct from those given to the people of Wadi Halfa. Although concerned about their future and the resettlement, the local ethnic groups were receiving their new neighbours with hospitality and on good terms (Dafalla 1975). Later on, during the first years of the scheme under operation, some conflict emerged with the farmers and the nomads regarding the feeding and watering of the camels and cattle. Even some cases of theft of cotton by the nomadic tribes were noted that escalated as high as 20 per cent of the total cotton production (Dafalla 1975). The pastoralists that were given tenancies in the scheme did not give up their pastoral activities but rather adapted their livelihood to include both pastoral and agricultural activities.

Although the sedentarisation of the nomadic tribes of the area was stated as one of the goals of the New Halfa agricultural scheme, its success has not been widely discussed or evaluated afterwards. In a Project Completion Report of the World Bank's *New Halfa Rehabilitation Project* (1992) it was stated that in 1978 out of the total estimated 300,000 residents of the scheme 68,000 were Halfawi and 148,000 were nomads. Considering the large percentage of the nomadic population in New Halfa they have been regarded as somewhat secondary and external to the scheme development. Despite the large share of the nomadic population there is little integration between the Halfawi and the nomads and they were settled separately (The World Bank 1992).

The relations between the Halfawi and the nomadic tribes were often based on labour recruitment and market exchange (Sørbø 1985). Despite incorporation into the same agricultural scheme, the livelihood patterns of Halfawi and the nomads remained different. Whereas the Halfawi would resort to other, often more urban, professions for extra income, the nomads would continue pasturing. It is also evident that the original structure of the scheme was unequal. The different premises and opportunities embedded the idea of differentiation among the various groups of the scheme and promoted unequal accumulation of wealth and capital. It is therefore understandable that the continuity of pastoralism was seen as a necessary source of income and a lifeline. There is a need for an integrated development plan that pays livestock more attention within agricultural schemes. Especially taking into account the fluctuation of the agricultural outputs, the livestock economy of the nomads – together with farming activities – could prove more rewarding (Abu Sin 1970).

7. For better or for worse: New Halfa today from the residents' perspective

In the following section the views of the residents in New Halfa today will be discussed to better understand the current condition of the scheme and the social and environmental risks of resettlement and state-driven development initiatives. The results presented below have been gathered through semi-constructed interviews and group discussions held in New Halfa, Sudan, in July-Agust 2011. The total amount of interviews, individual and group, was 29. The interviews were held in the centre of New Halfa and in the various villages around the scheme. However, due to the rainy season and the inaccessibility of the roads the farthest villages could not be reached. The ethnic groups of the interviewees were mainly Halfawi Nubians and nomadic or semi-nomadic, such as Shukriya, Zaghava, Rashaida and Hadendowa. In addition, migrant workers originating from western regions of Sudan, such as Darfur and the Nuba Mountains, were also interviewed. However, as the interviews could not be conducted systematically to evenly represent the different ethnic groups and the geographical locations of the villages, the results of the interviews are presented thematically under each heading.

7.1 Present conditions and challenges for the farmer in New Halfa

Many of the farmers interviewed owned 15 feddans of land according to the original resettlement plan; however some of the farmers had accumulated larger tenancies of up to 100 feddans. The most common crops they farmed were cotton, groundnuts, sorghum, wheat and to a smaller extent some seasonal fruit and vegetables. According to many farmers the scheme is encouraging the farming of cotton because of its high export value. However, the challenges expressed were lack of financial loans and difficulties in financing the high agricultural input, instability of crop prices and fluctuations in the market prices that create insecurity.

The managing body of the scheme, The New Halfa Agricultural Production Corporation (NHAPC), does give assistance for the farmers. However, some other residents who do not own land but work as labourers said that the scheme is not helping them. The people who live in the informal settlements receive less assistance. Through my personal visits to the NHAPC headquarters and discussions with the staff, I could sense their difficult position between the government and the farmers, and the constraints due to outdated resources and service facilities. The machinery available at the Scheme has deteriorated and has not been replaced and the NHAPC is not able to provide sufficient assistance to the farmers.

According to the respondents, the conditions for the farmers have deteriorated and at the same time they are increasingly dependent on external macro-economic factors and price fluctuations. In its almost 50 years of existence New

Halfa has witnessed environmental degradation through loss of land fertility and water contamination. The remaining part of arable land is under cultivation and the growth of cash crops such as cotton continues to be a major source of revenue for the state. Despite this, the benefits seldom reach the average farmer and their communities. The marginalisation of the tenants in the farming process is a result of the need to intensify land use against the land degradation and decreasing fertility, in order to meet the demands of agricultural inputs so they can receive better outputs (Robbins 2004). This places the farmers under pressure to sustain their livelihoods and makes them dependent on the price fluctuations in agricultural inputs and outputs.

According to the respondents there were differences to the extent that NHAPC has assisted them with problems related to farming. In addition to technical assistance the respondents complained about the increasing costs of farming and income insecurities. Some farmers have managed to become successful farmers; however most of the scheme residents have found that the scheme has not significantly improved their livelihoods. This accumulation of tenancies for fewer tenants is a sign of the failure of the scheme, as it was initially based on the principle of equal sized tenancies for all farmers. Especially for the semi-nomadic groups such as the Zaghava it is difficult to receive assistance from the scheme. The operational sustainability of the scheme is also under question as the maintenance of the scheme has proved inadequate. In numerous interviews the residents complained about the lack of maintenance of the canals. The quality of water is often poor and the inputs are increasingly high against the outputs. For many farmers the income from farming is not enough and they have to have other income sources to balance the costs.

7.2 Other livelihood means and income sources

Not all the respondents were farmers. Farming is still the main source of livelihood in New Halfa, but many respondents had multiple means of income. This often depends on the amount of land the farmer has. Besides being a farmer or working as a farm labourer many worked at the market in town. Some of the respondents were also government employees and agricultural experts. Most of the respondents who were satisfied with their income were farmers and Halfawi Nubians with their own land. Besides farming many Halfawi had other businesses in town or they hired farm labour for their tenancies while pursuing other careers. The respondents who were previously nomadic pastoralists were balancing between a lifestyle of nomadic cattle herding and more sedentary farming. According to the interviews nomadic people such as the Shukriya were more integrated into the farming lifestyle compared to the nomadic groups of Hadendowa, for instance. The people from western parts of Sudan had a wide variety of livelihoods according to the work available.

According to the respondents the livelihood sources are variable and differ between the ethnic groups. Although farming is the main source of livelihood other occupations have increasingly been taken to supplement the income from agriculture and to act as a buffer during times of small yields or low outputs. The scheme was based on the principle of 15 feddans per farmer but this is no longer the standard. Among the Nubians there is a high rate of absentee landlordism, where the farmers are able to pursue other occupations while the actual farm labour is being done by migrant workers and other landless farmers. Furthermore, the growing migration of the Halfawi Nubians to Khartoum has given the remaining Nubians the possibility to accummulate large shares of land in New Halfa.

Consequently, the town of New Halfa has become a significant regional trade and business hub and has created employment in various fields, from internet cafes to informal street vending. Therefore, in terms of income diversification the New Halfa scheme has succeeded in creating new business opportunities. The sugar factory and the other industrial activities nearby are also providing employment and income diversification for some. This, together with the opportunities for informal trade, has given many residents additional sources of income. Many local women, mainly from Beja-speaking ethnic groups, are selling handmade crafts and household items at the New Halfa market and this has given them an opportunity for an independent income. As urbanisation and changing lifestyles have also reached New Halfa, urban professions in finance, technology and computer-related businesses are creating even wider spatial differentiation in development between the urban core of the New Halfa town and its more educated citizens and the distant villages and the pastoralists on the peripheries who have limited chances to access the town. The local pastoralists, traditionally living around the New Halfa of today, still remain among the poorest and least healthy in Sudan (Cockett 2010).

Dependency on external factors has made it difficult for the farmers to rely on farming as their only source of income. The insecurities and fluctuations in global market prices have placed farmers in a very vulnerable position and therefore they are less resilient to the negative effects of global economic crises. The shift from traditional livelihood means and subsistence farming to a more capitalist mode of farming and finance has therefore had negative outcomes. Naturally this is not unique to New Halfa but is a globalised phenomenon. However, the scheme's focus on a few crops such as cotton, sorghum, wheat and groundnuts gives little flexibility and alternatives during times of low market prices for these crops. Additionally, the scheme does not allow diversification of agricultural practices or promote farmers' independence and initiative when it comes to decision-making.

During my field work in New Halfa I also observed the poor availability of food, especially vegetables, sold at the local market. The local street restaurants had little availability of food apart from the few staple meals. Although many residents grow vegetables for their own domestic consumption, the growth of cash crops may result in food shortages – especially in the areas with limited access to irrigation water.

Many of the local residents of the area have, because of the scheme, lost parts of their customary land and their traditional means of subsistence. Consequently, those who became tenants of the scheme lost their autonomy in agricultural decision making and influence in rural development (Salem-Murdock 1989:5). This evidently changed peoples' livelihoods and their position from independence and autonomy to being subject to the needs and requirements of the scheme. At the same time, some managed to accumulate tenancies and become landlords while others remained farm labourers with casual work. This caused economic differentiation and distribution of labour within the scheme that, for many, was an unfamiliar social order. The shift to the capitalist mode of production due to the scheme also transformed the peoples' assets, such as land, labour and livestock, into commodities (Salem-Murdock 1989:4). This gave some better positions and consequently made some inferior, such as the landless migrant workers.

The uneven development that is seen in New Halfa is a consequence of the different positions the new inhabitants had since the start of the scheme. It is the different ownership relationships in society and the social relations of reproduction that create the inequalities and on-going poverty in New Halfa (Gottdiener & Budd 2005). The disparity in financial assets between the different ethnic groups and communities, together with spatial differences are likely going to grow stronger. Salem-Murdock, among other scholars, also argues that the scheme has in fact widened the gap between the rich and the poor in the area (Salem-Murdock 1989). The residents are able to make a sufficient living only by generating income out of many tenancies or by having other sources of income in addition to farming.

Most of the nomadic groups interviewed have continued their pastoral practices and it seems a viable option, especially when the income from other sources is not sufficient. However, in respect of livelihood and income the migrant workers and internal refugees are the worst off, since they do not even have the asset of owning livestock or rights to customary land. Some of the migrants have lived in the scheme since the start and some have arrived more recently. Most of them live in informal settlements and have therefore limited access to resources and services. The people I interviewed for my study were working for the farms but did not own land of their own. Some had also businesses in town but out of the different ethnic and social groups within New Halfa the migrant labourers were in the most vulnerable position in terms of economic and social security.

7.3 Quality of water and environmental changes

Problems related to the quality of drinking water and the water in the canals emerged in all the interviews. The communities interviewed in and around the New Halfa scheme talked about problems with the quality of drinking water, to varying degrees. Water is taken from the canal and purified by using various traditional and modern methods. Some communities near the town of New Halfa have access to underground water. Access to water taps and purified water depends on the socio-economic status of the community. Whereas some nomadic groups now had better accessibility to water following the construction of the Khasm el Girba Dam and the canals many Nubians claimed water was better in the old Wadi Halfa. Water shortages seem to occur during summer months when the quality also deteriorates. Throughout the history of the scheme there have been several outbreaks of waterborne diseases due to contaminated water in the canals. It is presumably because the canals are regularly used for human bathing, cattle crossing and watering and increasingly infested by weeds (See figure 3.). The lack of sewage systems in the more informal settlements further contaminates the canals. The use of heavy fertilisers and pesticides can also contaminate the canals and make it toxic for human consumption.

According to the interviews, people living in informal settlements and nomadic temporary settlements do not pay for the water but use it freely from the canals. The original housing provided by the scheme has water storage with chlorine purification from where the water runs through the taps. However the system is old and needs maintenance. Diseases occur more in informal settlements where there is no adequate water purification. The lack of sewer and human waste management, particularly in the informal and semi-nomadic settlements, has contaminated and polluted the canals through run-off and drainage. This has led to serious outbreaks of waterborne diseases such as malaria, bilharzia and diarrhea that continue to be prevalent within the scheme. However there are differences in water availability and quality between the villages. The best situation is within the town of New Halfa and in the villages within the infrastructure network. These are mostly the villages of the Halfawi Nubians that were constructed by the government. However the Nubians have also complained about the deteriorating state of the water purification stations as many are in need of maintenance.

Within the informal and nomadic villages the water is mostly carried from the canals and purified using traditional methods of stone/sand filtration or using plants such as *Moringa Oleifera*. Some villages also received chlorine tablets for water purification but many complained about the bad taste. Due to this, those who have limited access to purified water and have to utilise it straight from the canals are at a higher risk of falling ill with waterborne diseases and consequently in an even more disadvantaged position.

Figure 3. The canals are being used for human and animal washing (Wallin 2011).

The issue of rights to land and its resources has also become contested, as the same resources are now shared between a growing number of people. The landless people from Western Sudan have come as refugees or migrant workers but have no access to land of their own. The nomadic pastoralists have had to settle with less pastoral land and in addition the access to water resources for livestock watering has become limited. Access to land is therefore highly unequal and the traditional pastoral territories have been disregarded. Therefore, the socio-physical environment of New Halfa has been altered and transformed. The traditional territories have not been acknowledged by the government and consequently the allocation of rights and access to environmental resources has been altered. This is demonstrated in the process where the resettled Halfawi Nubians have been able to access and utilise the resources to a better extent than the local ethnic groups, who have also, at least partially, lost their customary rights to land.

The increasing demand for higher agricultural outputs has put pressure on the sustainability and fertility of arable land. In addition the whole of the New Halfa scheme relies on the regular flow of the River Atbara and the functionality of the Khasm el Girba dam. The increased sedimentation due to upstream run-off has decreased the storage capacity, and the water flow to the scheme canals has been disturbed. Some farmers claim that the water does not always reach the farmlands in the northernmost parts of the scheme.

The increased production pressure and competition on resources will seriously affect the environmental sustainability of the New Halfa scheme and its future productivity. The Tekeze dam on the Tekeze River that joins the Atbara River will alleviate the problem of sedimentation and the source of water for irrigation is therefore sustainable. However, the access to water resources within the scheme should be socially more equal and regionally balanced. Partial covering of the canal could decrease the water contamination and evaporation and investments in communal water purification stations and communal water taps could help control the outbreaks of diseases. The scheme continues to rely on the government for financial assistance and lack of funds seems to be the underlying cause for the lack of water infrastructure maintenance.

7.4 Housing, infrastructure and services

The villages near the New Halfa town are generally well established with formal housing, roads and services nearby. The close proximity to the town gives better access to services such as schools and the New Halfa hospital. The villages further away have less access to services, especially during the rainy season when the roads become muddy thus making transportation nearly impossible. The available infrastructure also depends on the original layout of the residential areas and villages. The resettled Halfawi Nubians received ready-built houses in villages with roads, electricity and water storage as compensation for their relocation. The Shukriya were given land but many had to build their own houses. Many of the informal settlements are inhabited by wage labour workers from other parts of Sudan or nomadic pastoralists from the region that have settled in the scheme (See figures 4–6.). The informal settlements fall outside of the

Figure 4. A Halfawi Nubian village (Wallin 2011).

Resettled for Development

Figure 5. A Beja village (Wallin 2011).

Figure 6. An informal settlement for migrant workers, IDPs and landless people (Wallin 2011).

infrastructure network and most of them have no electricity, road connections or services. Many informal settlements have been established for a long time but they are waiting to be registered officially. Although the houses of the Halfawi are built by the government and have adequate infrastructure surrounding them, they have started to deteriorate and show problems. The houses that were built by the scheme have roofs made out of poisonous asbestos. This used to be a valuable building material, however it was later discovered to cause health problems for the residents.

It is evident that the scheme cannot keep up with the demand for services and due to the limited financial support from the government the infrastructure remains outdated and insufficient. For the sustainability of the scheme it would be essential to support the services and infrastructure so that outbreaks of diseases could be controlled and residents could have access to health and educational services, irrespective of the location of their villages. It would also be important to better acknowledge the permanent presence of the migrant workers which is benefiting the agricultural system through the supply of a workforce. There is a drastic difference between the living conditions and service sector of the Halfawi and central Shukriya villages and the informal settlements of the semi-nomadic groups and migrants. Although the infrastructure was generally outdated within all of the villages visited for this study, in many informal settlements the complete lack of infrastructure placed its residents in a very vulnerable position in terms of lacking the basic human needs such as provision of clean water, housing, health services and accessibility.

7.5 Equality and integration

The question of social equality and integration in New Halfa is contested as, right from the start, circumstances have varied between different communities. The displaced Nubian Halfawi were resettled in their own villages with houses and tenancies as compensation for their loss. Other nomadic groups were also given tenancies but not all received housing. Some other nomadic groups of people from the region joined the scheme later due to sedentarisation policies and better access to services and markets. Inequality exists among different villages and it continues to fragment the scheme.

The respondents highlighted the big differences between the villages. Among members of other ethnic groups a sense of bitterness towards the Halfawi Nubians was expressed. Their better living conditions do not seem justifiable to others when almost 50 years have passed since the resettlement. The ingrained inequalities have further abated social integration and contact between different ethnic groups. Since the start of the scheme, social and economic differentiation has existed and promoted unequal accumulation of wealth and tenancies. The resettlement of the Halfawi Nubians gave them a feeling of entitlement and exceptionality, as if the scheme was there to only compensate for their loss. The choice of naming the scheme *New Halfa* already supported this outlook and the superior position of the Halfawi within the scheme. Because of this the Halfawi Nubians were reluctant to interact with the other residents and rather chose to continue living in isolation. It is probable that this sense of alienation was also caused by the lack of feeling of attachment and belonging to New Halfa, and this led to further resentment.

Some of the local nomadic tribes were also sedentarised and incorporated into the scheme, however with less benefits and opportunities. Many of them chose to continue their pastoral livelihoods for primary or additional income. This caused conflict with the Nubians over access to pastoral land and over the entry of livestock to farmlands. Most of the migrant labour that arrived before the Nubian resettlement to construct the scheme's housing and urban facilities is still residing at New Halfa, some better off than others, but most of them living in unregistered shanty towns without proper infrastructure, such as running water or social services. Whereas many Nubians are now able to practice other professions besides managing their tenancies, many migrants are working as seasonal farmers on land they do not own. The living conditions of the farm workers and migrants can be described as desolate and excluded. As many of the migrant workers that now reside within the scheme have had to settle for whatever land is left available, they are often residing in areas with limited connectivity and mostly non-existing service availability. The fact that they only interact with other scheme residents in the form of subordinate work relationships or trade in the market leaves little possibility for neutral and equal interaction.

Despite the difficult conditions the migrant workers from areas of West and South Sudan have settled to the different environment of Eastern Sudan well. This is most likely due to impossible conditions in the conflict areas of Darfur and Nuba Mountains that worked as push-factors and to the fact that they came to New Halfa by choice in hope of a better life. However, the Halfawi Nubians were generally treating them with uneasiness, doubt and avoidance (Haydar 2008). This is most likely due to the feeling of entitlement to the scheme that is still prevalent among Halfawi and the reluctance to share the limited resources with the ever-growing population.

The interview results for this study did not indicate major conflict between the Nubians and the migrant workers. However, no social contact or relationships were mentioned between the Halfawi and other ethnic groups and the isolation of the different groups was tangible. The possible conflict scenarios are disputes over access to natural resources and over limited social services. According to the people in one of the informal settlements near the town of New Halfa, the children go to the school in the nearby village and the water is collected from the canals despite the fact that they are not officially registered as residents of the scheme and do not pay for the water as the other registered residents do. Therefore conflicts arise when limited resources and territories are being utilised by groups with different levels of entitlement, not because of ethnic or cultural disputes.

Different livelihoods or exclusive social organisation can, to some extent, explain the divide, conflict and lack of integration between the different ethnic groups within New Halfa. However, as the interviews conducted during the field work point out, there are different levels of entitlement, access to resources and services between the residents. The entrenched social differentiation within the scheme caused the formation of power hierarchies between the different residents as some managed to accumulate a large amount of tenancies and the others could not improve their livelihoods through farm wage labour. The result of this unequal treatment between the relocated Nubians and the host Arabs was increasing ethnic seclusion (Salem-Murdock 1989). The interviews and observations conducted for this study concur with this statement and the situation seems unchanged.

The fluctuating macro-economic conditions, deteriorating environmental resources and the policies that neglect rural development have led to increased conflicts that are often based on livelihood needs. This has not been improved by the New Halfa scheme that implemented unequal land-tenure systems and placed some at an advantage in comparison to other residents. The fact that the residents were situated in different villages according to ethnic origin further embedded the idea of differentiation and segregation within the scheme.

8. Victims or beneficiaries of development?

The last section will discuss New Halfa as a project of Nubian resettlement and the sedentarisation of nomadic groups and conclude to what extent it succeeded in this goal. According to many scholars it appears that the New Halfa scheme has failed to meet most of its target goals and has not significantly contributed towards the development of its residents' livelihoods. Although New Halfa has, in general, contributed towards the wider national economy through crop exports and revenue it has also made the tenants more dependent on the cash crop price fluctuations and the global economy. In terms of global capitalism the tenants can be seen as subordinate agricultural producers who have no say in what to grow and how to grow it, and yet the financial gains of their work do not trickle down to the farmers.

New Halfa has also witnessed a decrease in the equity of resource distribution. The income inequity emerged since the start of the scheme and, despite the more modern means of agricultural production, the overall sustainability of the scheme is under question. The declining state of the environment and the growing need of extraction or utilisation of natural resources can also be expected to be seen among the most marginalised and poorest in the communities. The farmers are on the periphery when it comes to power and decision-making and they often lack capital and a financial buffer during economic hardship. Thus, they have little alternative but to overexploit natural resources.

In the original masterplan the equal sized tenancies of each farmer should have been enough to support the livelihood of the farmer and their families. However, this failed from the start and supported the economic differentiation that began to emerge within the scheme. Farmers started to accumulate land and take measures into their own hands. Although the scheme tried to control this, the growth of an elite minority of well-off farmers could not be stopped (Salem-Murdock 1989). Although some, mainly Shukriya farmers, were allocated farming land most of the nomads did not receive tenancies. This enabled the more well-off farmers to increase their profits as workforce was easily available and they could afford the machinery and fertilisers that were needed to maximise the profits. Although this discriminated against the poorer tenants it also gave many a reason to stay within the scheme. On the other hand, the poor return from agriculture for some encouraged the growth of the urban sector within the town of New Halfa. This has created a substantial amount of professions and new forms of business that were not anticipated in the planning of the scheme (Salem-Murdock 1989). The fact that the planners of the scheme did not pay attention to individual differentiation and the right of decision of the farmers was one of the factors that contributed to the failure of the scheme as a development initiative. Therefore, it was only through these individual choices and actions that the scheme became beneficial for some of its tenants. The importance of self-determination and empowerment within development initiatives therefore cannot be overemphasised.

The New Halfa scheme did improve the livelihood conditions for some who managed to accumulate land and assets, but on the other hand those left with small tenancies struggled to the extent that some decided to leave the scheme. Some of the nomads, the landless migrant workers and IDPs were also in a disadvantaged position and had to settle for the work they were able to find without having their own tenancies. The varying distribution of economic assets and opportunities within the scheme has promoted further segregation and disputes between the residents. The relationships that are limited to those between tenants and wage workers do not provide a favourable setting for equal social intercourse. Therefore, the fact that those who were displaced due to development were compensated and those displaced due to conflict were not shows the problem of the role of the state being both the violator of rights and arbiter of justice (Assal 2008). The focus should be more on securing the rights of all displaced people despite their background, and the cases of forced migration should be dealt with comprehensively. However, the basic rights of IDPs have been neglected in Sudan for a long period of time due to discriminatory policies and for political reasons. The question of identity and the climate of politicised Islam have further complicated matters (Assal 2008).

In the case of New Halfa, there is therefore a need to realise the equal rights of all its residents, and the migrant labourers and IDPs should be seen as important assets of agricultural workforce that are the prerequisites of continuity and sustainability of the scheme. For those coming from conflict regions with their livelihoods disrupted New Halfa has been able to offer a chance to improve their situations. The fact that many of them have come to New Halfa by choice is also an important factor to consider when other groups, such as the Halfawi, are still bearing the trauma of forced displacement.

Therefore, although New Halfa was not, overall, a successful development project it did result in some residents improving their own economic situations and income generation – something that would not have taken place without the scheme. However, the state's one-sided view of development contradicted with the local livelihoods. Those who did not adhere to this imposed idea of development were left with fewer possibilities for alternative development strategies. Consequently, development that is coerced has little chance of sustaining itself and if any lessons can be learnt, it is crucial to incorporate the beneficiaries in the planning process of development projects and to acknowledge the possibilities and consequences of economic and social differentiation.

8.1 New Halfa as a showcase of resettlement of the Halfawi Nubians

The outcome of a development initiative that includes a human component is always difficult to predict, and despite careful planning the external impacts may redirect the course and cause unforeseen challenges. Although the planning and implementation process of the resettlement of the Halfawi Nubians was thoroughly thought out, especially in terms of practical arrangements and compensation (Dafalla 1975), it did not succeed in its goal of engineering new social territories. The above mentioned results have shown the degree of resentment and withdrawal by the Halfawi Nubians and the emerging economic differentiation between the resettled and the host population due to unequal compensation. In the future the Halfawi Nubians within New Halfa will be an increasing minority and the already established multi-ethnic communities of mixed origin will have to be better incorporated into the scheme to secure its sustainability.

As Philip Woodhouse (1988:29) states, "irrigation systems are designed by engineers, operated by agriculturalists and evaluated by social scientists" without really communicating with each other and sharing their knowledge. There are strong arguments for and against, and the debate whether dams should be built or not is likely to remain unsettled. Hence, the fact that dams are increasingly being built and people consequently resettled calls for a holistic approach that combines the work of engineers, agriculturalists, social scientist and the people involved, in order to better plan the development initiatives. It must be understood that without including the communities at stake in the planning process, the development and resettlement projects are unlikely to be sustainable and successful.

If we go back to the resettlement of the Nubians that happened almost 50 years ago it can be stated that the displacement altered their lives significantly and irreversibly. The Halfawi Nubians lost their previous livelihoods, territory, historical entitlement to their land, patterns and networks of social organisation and much of their sense of belonging. The fact that they were not adequately consulted about the resettlement, and the place of resettlement was decided against their choice shows a lack in acknowledging the negative social impact that dam constructions and top-down development initiatives continue to have. Although the Halfawi were compensated for their displacement in many ways, they were not incorporated into the planning of the resettlement and their future role was seen as mere producers of agricultural revenue for the state.

If we discuss the eight risks of the impoverishment, risks and reconstruction (IRR) model (*landlessness, joblessness, homelessness, marginalisation, increased morbidity and mortality, food insecurity, loss of access to common resources and services and social or communal disarticulation* (Cernea 2005)), the issue of landlessness and social or communal disarticulation have been heavily experienced by the Halfawi Nubians. The compensation did not substitute the customary ownership of land in Wadi Halfa or pay justice to the loss of cultural land of old Nubia where they, in many ways, felt a sense of 'belonging'. Therefore, the loss of cultural identity and material livelihoods is a risk that has potentially led to impoverishment of the Halfawi Nubians in New Halfa (Cernea 2005). On the other hand, the risks of joblessness, homelessness, increased morbidity and mortality and food insecurity were counteracted by giving the Halfawi Nubians a tenancy to cultivate as a profession, a home to settle in, health and educational services and freehold land for personal subsistence farming. Therefore they received a relatively secure source of livelihood, at least during the first decades of the scheme when the land was still fertile and the yields sufficient.

Due to the compensation the Nubians received, they are today some of the most well-off residents in New Halfa. This is not, however, only because of the compensation but also because of the many Halfawi who left the scheme and allowed the remaining Nubians to accumulate their tenancies and become landlords that hire farm labour, which enables them to seek additional income sources, often more urban professions. The risks of social and communal disarticulation also materialised to the extent that the original kinship-based communities were largely dispersed and many cultural traditions lost in the transition. The shift from self-determined, partly subsistence, farming to a large irrigation scheme where the crops were chosen by the management also led to a lack of ownership and commitment by the Halfawi. The fact that they became the subjects of the resettlement rather than being proactive contributors with the power of decision, to some extent paralysed them, and caused withdrawal from the scheme. Therefore this can also be seen as a materialisation of the Sudanese ruling elite, using their political and territorial power to violate the territorial dignity of the Nubians and to reduce them to the status of farmers in New Halfa, whose task, above all, is to provide revenue for the state.

Sudan has not succeeded in the equitable use of natural resources and the centralised power elite continue to control the economy and territories by making decisions on behalf of the stakeholders, such as the farmers, leaving people without the right to decide over their own livelihoods (Abdalla 2008). Therefore, this eventually leads to further political and territorial marginalisation of the Nubians and other residents of the scheme. The resettlement of the Nubians was however successful in theory and partly during the first operational years of the scheme. When the New Halfa scheme was constructed its farming technology was modern: large-scale irrigation systems, urban services and advanced infrastructure. The town of New Halfa was designed by engineers and the canal layout was very modern compared to Wadi Halfa. However, the quickly deteriorating conditions and the changes in the agricultural inputs and outputs forced many to look for additional sources of income and some to leave the scheme.

The amount of research done on the increasing differentiation and diversification of livelihoods in New Halfa is also a sign of the failure of tenancy farming in being an adequate source of income for the tenants (Sørbø 1985; Salem-Murdock 1989). Although some were able to economically benefit from the scheme there is no evidence that the resettlement raised the overall living standards of the majority in the scheme (Salem-Murdock 1989; Haydar 2008). It is therefore often stated that resettlement projects are one of the least satisfactory of development interventions. It also undermines the importance and possibilities of indigenous systems of production and superimposes the ideals of the modern capitalistic modes of production for development (Haydar 2008).

This system failed to create wealth for the farmers in New Halfa. The ones who managed to make a living succeeded in this by accumulating tenancies, having off-scheme businesses in the town of New Halfa or elsewhere or continued with pastoral livelihoods. This is contrary to the original operational principle of the scheme and goes to show the failure in meeting the aims of the scheme. The planners did not consider the individual choices, farming methods and differentiation between the farmers and did not include them in the planning and implementation process. The failure of the resettlement was therefore the lack of understanding the importance of inclusive participatory planning that eventually resulted in lack of attachment and ownership from the residents' side.

8.2 The situation of the nomadic groups in New Halfa

The nomadic groups, with the exception of some representatives of the Shukriya semi-nomadic group, were generally worse off than their Nubian counterparts according to observation. Many of them lived outside the infrastructure network and in villages that were not officially registered as part of the scheme. When visited during the rainy season some of the villages had become completely inaccessible and some of the houses constructed of natural materials had been damaged due to the rainy and wet conditions. However, the most visible difference was the lack of infrastructure and services. The Shukriya were the most well-off in terms of housing and sufficient income from cultivation. However, within the Shukriya there are big differences in terms of income and benefits. Salem-Murdock speaks of a special Shukriya elite, that include particularly those with lineages associated with the traditional rulers, who have profited greatly from involvement in the scheme. As a consequence, the gap between the rich and poor Shukriya has widened (Salem-Murdock 1989:12).

The other nomadic groups, such as Rashaida, Hadendowa and Zaghava are generally economically deprived and have little personal assets. The nomadic groups in the scheme had fewer benefits from the start. Although the scheme originally gave the Shukriya and other nomadic groups of the region farming possibilities in the form of tenancies, the nomadic villages were situated further away from the town of New Halfa and often lacked the same services as the Nubian villages. The availability of education and health services undoubtedly improved living standards and gave opportunities for many nomads. However, the quality of services deteriorated and due to the loss of fertility in the land and water shortages the nomadic groups continued with their pastoral livelihoods. The negative consequences of the scheme for the nomads were the decrease in the pastoral and migration land for their livestock as well as the increase in waterborne diseases.

The nomadic groups were given some benefits, such as the 15 feddan of land to cultivate per tenant, but many chose to continue their pastoral livelihoods in addition to farming as it remained an important source of income and independence (Sørbø 1977; Sørbø 1985). It is evident that due to the establishment of the New Halfa irrigation scheme parts of the traditional Butana grazing land had been appropriated by the state, exercising their control over the traditional territories of indigenous groups. Therefore, as discussed in the context of political ecology, the environmental changes directed by the state have politicised the environment and altered the social construction of the socio-physical relations within the region. The territorial rights of the nomadic groups of people have been the target of intervention by the dominant political group that has overruled their rights – as irrigation schemes were seen as a better, more productive, method of land use (Yong Ooi Lin 2008). Therefore, the environmental transformation that took place in New Halfa was part of the economic and political context of that time and also manifested the hegemony of the Sudanese political core and its attempt to mainstream and uniform the ethnic fabric of Sudan to the extent that it undermines the rights of ethnic minorities (Paulson et al. 2003) .

Hence, the construction of the Aswan High Dam by Egypt, the displacement that followed and the construction of the New Halfa irrigation scheme have all been part of the overall agenda to modernise and develop the region but have also changed the social structure of entitlement to natural resources. Although the displacement of the Sudanese Nubians was caused by Egypt's need to secure their share of the Nile waters, the New Halfa resettlement project also fit into Sudan's objective of promoting national integration and state-directed social change by incorporating both the previously isolated Halfawi Nubians and the independent and mobile nomadic groups into the irrigation scheme.

It has been stated that development projects tend to displace and target indigenous and marginalised ethnic groups as they are often seen as undeveloped, loose and therefore a hindrance to national unity. Furthermore, these projects tend to make them lose their own social networks and strategies of development (Yong Ooi Lin 2008). As the indigenous groups are not always aware of their rights as a citizen they may also lack the necessary skills to protect their rights to their customary lands. In the context of land ownership and territorialism this is particularly difficult, as the nomadic pastoralists have regarded the land as common property and have consequently lacked experience in exercising decision-making power. Moreover, the Unregistered Land Act of 1970 left many traditional ethnic groups without rights to the land they had utilised (Eskonheimo 2006). This can have many detrimental consequences to their sense of belonging, community structure and livelihood methods.

Pastoralism was never really supported by the government as its contribution to the national economy was seen as non-existant and the pastoral lifestyle as backward. The situation of the nomadic groups is problematic as they are politically and socially marginalised, yet their lifestyle can in many ways contribute to food production in the region. They receive little assistance from the government or the scheme unless they abandon some of their pastoral lifestyles and sedentarise as farmers. With the current unattractive situation of the New Halfa scheme this seems unlikely to happen. The independence, flexibility and sustainability of pastoralism seems to be too erratic to fall under government control. On the other hand, as the customary pastoral territories continue to decrease, the nomadic groups, sooner or later, have no choice but to adapt their lifestyles and incorporate into the Sudanese economy.

The treatment of the nomadic groups as secondary by the state officials in the planning and implementation of the scheme and the deteriorating agricultural conditions have encouraged most of the nomadic groups to continue engaging in pastoral activities to at least a certain extent. Some have managed to accumulate farming land and have become completely ex-nomadic or semi-nomadic However, the majority tend to continue benefiting from pastoralism as livestock remains a viable source of income and security, especially considering the uncertain prospects for agriculture in New Halfa.

8.3 Future prospects for New Halfa and Sudanese agriculture

With the increasing demand for energy and 'more crop for drop' Sudan will continue to follow the trend of hydro-engineering within the Nile basin. The growing demand for the Nile waters, particularly due to the population growth in the region and the increasing hydro-engineering in Ethiopia, may cause disputes and strain the relations between the Nile basin countries. Sudan has not yet fully utilised its share of the waters, as stated in the 1959 Nile Waters Agreement, and is therefore currently initiating new dam projects and irrigation schemes. Although the water scarcity will likely hit Egypt the hardest, Sudan has embarked on a mission to develop the water-infrastructure in the northern parts of the country. New dams will lay the suitable groundwork for more irrigated agriculture and consequently more people will be displaced.

The future prospects for New Halfa are challenging to outline. The Halfawi

Nubians continue to migrate out of the scheme and the younger generation seem more attracted to urban professions and possibilities. The nomadic groups will likely continue with their pastoral practices and participate in farming according to opportunities. The continuing flow of migrant workers and internally displaced people from other parts of Sudan will play an increasingly important role in the future of the scheme and alter its social composition. A large number will engage with farming activities and work as farm labourers. However, the town of New Halfa has become a significant urban centre and will offer more possibilities for entrepreneurs and the informal sector.

One of the challenges of combining social resettlement and irrigation schemes as a development project is the difficulty in considering the future prospects. How will the host population and the resettled population integrate and promote the development of the scheme? When will the resettled become settled and the legacy, or burden, of resettlement left in the past? It is difficult to estimate the lifespan of a resettlement project and the time required for an irrigation scheme to become self-sustaining. It is also relevant to ask whether the government of Sudan should continue to be held responsible for a resettlement that took place 50 years ago, and remain responsible for problems that have emerged in the scheme since its establishment. However, some of the social problems within the scheme can be explained by the challenges of regulating the livelihoods of its farmers and the promotion of unequal development. The social and economic differentiation is continuing to fragment the scheme. The nomadic host population have not been adequately incorporated into the scheme and as a consequence they have not been enticed to leave their pastoral practices. For the future it is important to consider the rights and preferences of the nomads and acknowledge the economic benefits of pastoralism as a sustainable land use pattern. However, as the Sudanese policies have favoured large-scale agricultural development the value of the local environmental knowledge is threatened.

9. Conclusion

As the example of New Halfa illustrates, the development-induced displacement of people is often not considered thoroughly as a process with long-term effects and an irreversible negative impact on the self-determination and integrity of the targeted group of people. This eventually became detrimental to the scheme as the Halfawi Nubians never became rooted and attached to their new home in New Halfa. The resettlement gave them an advantage in terms of compensation and a sense of entitlement and superiority within the scheme. This consequently left the rest of the scheme residents with less benefits and opportunities, although they were the majority of the New Halfa agricultural scheme. Furthermore, the challenges of New Halfa, in terms of land degradation and loss of irrigation water became evident soon after the start. The poor agricultural revenue proved a disappointment to the government and the local people and despite the rehabilitation attempts the scheme never reached its original targets of productivity. Some of the Halfawi Nubians left the scheme as some accumulated tenancies and became landlords while pursuing other businesses. Nomadic groups never abandoned their pastoral practices completely as they proved to be an important source of income and independence. In the later years the scheme suffered from serious outbreaks of waterborne diseases and deterioration in the service and infrastructure within the scheme.

Today the scheme is operating within the limits of the available irrigation water with means that contradict the original principles of equal sized tenancies. The economic differentiation within the scheme is increasing and the residents remain in their segregated villages as in the original residential plan. The migrant workers, internal refugees from West Sudan and the newly settled nomadic groups reside in informal settlements such as shanty towns that are excluded from the infrastructure and service sector. They are increasing in number and will possibly become the major workforce within the scheme in the future.

However, considering the challenges and the overall climate of conflict that Sudan has faced over the past decades, it is important not to look at the development of New Halfa in isolation. Despite the fact that the scheme is lacking an adequate service sector and fails to provide enough income for the tenants, it has become the destination for many Sudanese throughout the country in search of better life opportunities.

The Halfawi Nubians were forced to relocate to New Halfa and are thus still experiencing feelings of nostalgia for their traditional homeland in the old Nubia. The unpleasantness of forced displacement together with the passive dependence and lack of ownership within the irrigation scheme can to some extent explain the outflow of the Nubian farmers from New Halfa. However, the present challenges in the scheme cannot be solely blamed on the resettlement that took place 50 years ago. As with other development projects, the goal is to eventually create independence and sustainability and the residents should become active participants in the management and future planning of the scheme.

Understanding that dams change the landscape greatly but also affect the livelihoods of thousands of people receives much attention; however, little remains done to mitigate the negative risks of resettlement caused by dams. The displacement and uprooting of the Nubians from Wadi Halfa has been seen as an attempt at social engineering by the government and the Sudanese political elite's way of exercising their territorial power and hegemony against the minority ethnic groups within Sudan. Sudan continues to build new dams on the River Nile with disregard to the guidelines laid out by international organisations. The debate over dams seems to have been juxtaposed between those who acclaim dams as endless generators of development and prosperity and those who stress the negative environmental and social consequences. Dams continue to be built and to produce significant amounts of sustainable hydroelectric energy. Indeed, irrigation schemes as one of the products of dam construction and as destinations of resettlement can substantially promote the food security for the growing population and economic growth for the nation. Largely, though, they seem to fail to meet their targets. Including the people affected as beneficiaries of this development and as active participants in the implementation process may mitigate the negative performance of the scheme. More importantly, this can only be achieved if the rights of people to choose and direct their livelihoods are respected and secured.

References

Abdalla, M. (2008). Poverty and inequality in urban Sudan. Policies, institutions and governance. African Studies Centre, Netherlands.

Abdelrazig, E.M. (1979). Labor Requirements and Supply for Cotton Picking with Special Reference to Tenant Family Labor in New Halfa Agricultural Corporation – Sudan. Department of Agricultural Economics, Michigan State University.

Abu Sin, M.E. (1970). The Regional Geography of the Butana north of the Railway. Unpublished M.A. thesis, University of Khartoum, Sudan.

Adar K., (2001). Ethno-religious Nationalism in Sudan: The Enduring Constraint on the Policy of National identity. In: Bekker S., Dodds M. and Khosa M. (eds.), Shifting African Identities, pp. 81–113. Human Sciences Research Council, Pretoria.

Ahmad, M. & Abu Sin, H. (1990). Urban Development in a Rural Context: The Case of New Halfa, Sudan. In Small Town Africa, Studies in Rural-Urban Interaction. Ed. Baker, J. The Scandinavian Institute of African Studies, Seminar Proceedings No. 23. Uppsala.

Ahmed, A. (2001). Livelihood and Resource Competition, Sudan. African Pastoralism. Conflict, Institutions and Government. Ed. Salih, M., Dietz, T. and Ahmed, A. Pluto Press, USA.

Ahmed, A. (2002). Changing Systems of Livelihood in Rural Sudan. Organization for Social Science Research in Eastern and Southern Africa. Addis Ababa, Ethiopia.

Ahmed, M. (2009). Economic and Managerial implications for the Siltation in Khasm el Girba Dam Reservoir on New Halfa Agricultural Production Corporation – Sudan. A doctoral thesis. Department of Agricultural Economics, Faculty of Agriculture, University of Khartoum, Sudan.

Assal, M. (2008). Rights and Decisions to Return: Internally Displaced Persons in Post-war Sudan. In Forced Displacement: Why Rights Matter. Ed. Grabska, K. & Mehta, L. Palgrave Macmillan, UK.

Barraclough, S., Ghimire, K., Meliczek, H. (1997). Rural Development and the Environment. Towards Ecologically and Socially Sustainable Development in Rural Areas. UNRISD & UNEP, Switzerland.

Biong Deng, L. (2005). The Challenge of Cultural, Ethnic and Religious Diversity in Peacebuilding and Constitution-Making in Post-Conflict Sudan. Civil Wars, Vol. 7, No.3 pp. 258–269

Boege, V. & Turner, M. (2006). *Access to freshwater and Conflict Prevention, Management and Resolution in Africa.* In: Conflict Prevention, Management and Reduction in Africa: A Joint Project of the Finnish Institute of International Affairs & the Centre for International Cooperation and Security. Ed: Owen Greene, Julia Buxton and Charly Salonius-Pasternak. Hakapaino, Helsinki.

Cernea, M. (2005). Concept and Method: Applying the IRR Model in Africa to Resettlement and Poverty. In Displacement Risks in Africa. Refugees, Resettlers and Their Host Population. Ed. Ohta, I. & Gebre, Y. (2005) Kyoto University Press, Japan.

Cernea, M. (1995). Understanding and Preventing Impoverishment from Displacement: Reflections on the State of Knowledge. Journal of Refugee Studies Vol. 8, No. 3. 1995.

Chesworth, P. M. (1990). The history of Water Use in Sudan and Egypt. Paper presented at the Conference on the Nile convened at the Royal Geographical Society and at the University of London in May 1990.

Cockett, Richard (2010). Sudan: Darfur and the failure of an African state. Yale University Press.

Collins, R. (2008). Managing the Water of the Nile: Basis for Cooperation? Narrating the Nile, Politics, Cultures, Identities. Edited by Gershoni, I. & Hatina, M. Lynne Rienner Publishers Colorado. Pp. 181–201.

Collins, Robert (1990). History, Hydropolitics, and the Nile: Nile Control: Myth or Reality? Paper presented at the Conference on the Nile convened at the Royal Geographical Society and at the University of London in May 1990.

Dafalla, Hassan (1975). The Nubian Exodus. C. Hurst & Co. London.

Delaney, D. (2005): Territory. A Short Introduction. Blackwell, Malden. MA.

El Arifi, S. (1988). Problems in planning extensive agricultural projects: the case of New Halfa, Sudan. Applied Geography, 1988, 8, pp.37–52.

Eskonheimo, A. (2006). Women, environmental changes and forestry-related development: Gender-affected roles of rural people in land degradation and environmental rehabilitation in a dry region of Sudan. In: Tropical Forestry Reports; 29. Viikki Tropical Resources Institute. University of Helsinki.

Gottdiener, M. & Budd, L. (2005). Key Concepts in Urban Studies. Sage Publications, USA.

Gourbesville, P. (2008). Challenges for integrated water resources management. Physics and Chemistry of the Earth. Vol. 33, 284–289.

Government of Sudan and the World Bank (2000). Sudan. Options for the Sustainable Development of the Gezira Scheme.

Grabska, K. & Mehta, L. (2008). Forced Displacement. Why Rights Matter. Palgrave Macmillan, Great Britain.

Hashim, M. (2010) The dams of Northern Sudan and the policy of demographic engineering, International Journal of African Renaissance Studies – Multi-, Inter- and Transdisciplinarity, 5:1, 148–160

Haydar, H. (2008). The Social Cost of Resettlement: The Case of Halfawiyyin at Suburban Khartoum. A thesis submitted for the requirement of PhD in Social Anthropology. University of Khartoum, Sudan.

Hoag, H. (2013) Developing the Rivers of East and West Africa: An Environmental History. Bloomsbury Academic, United Kingdom.

Idris, Amir. (2005). Conflicts and Politics of Identity in Sudan. Palgrave Macmillan, England.

International Rivers Network (2013). Kajbar Dam, Sudan. http://www.international-rivers.org/campaigns/kajbar-dam-sudan 5.9.2013

International Rivers Network (2013). Merowe Dam, Sudan. *http://www.international-rivers.org/campaigns/merowe-dam-sudan-0 28.8.2013*

Jok, J. (2007). Sudan: Race, Religion, and Violence. Oneworld Publications, Oxford.

Kibreab, G. (2008). Access to Economic and Social Rights in First Countries of Asylum and Repatriation: a Case Study of Eritrean Refugees in Sudan. In Forced Displacement: Why Rights Matter. Ed. Grabska, K. & Mehta, L. Palgrave Macmillan, UK.

Laxen, J. (2007). Is prosopis a curse or a blessing? – An ecological-economic analysis of an invasive alien tree species in Sudan. Academic dissertation, University of Helsinki.

Minoia, P. (2012). Mega-irrigation and neoliberalism in post-colonial states: evolution and crisis in the Gharb Plain, Morocco. Geografiska Annaler: Series B, Human Geography 94 (3):1–18.

Morvaridi, B. (2008). Rights and Development-Induced Displacement: Risk Management or Social Protection? Forced Displacement; Why Rights Matter. Ed: Grabska, K. & Mehta, L. Palgrave Macmillan, Great Britain.

Natter, W. & Zierhofer, W. (2002). Political ecology, territoriality and scale. In Geojournal 58, pp. 225–231. Netherlands.

NHAPC (2011) Information gathered in the interviews with the staff of the New Halfa Agricultural (Production) Corporation, Sudan.

Nixon, R. (2010). Unimagined Communities: Developmental Refugees, Megadams and Monumental Modernity. In: New Formations, Vol. 69; pp. 62–80. Lawrence and Wishart Publications.

Oestigaard, T. (2012). Water Scarcity and Food Security along the Nile. Politics, population increase and climate change. Current African Issues, Vol. 49. Nordiska Afrikainstitutet, Uppsala.

Omer, A.M. (2007). Water Resources and freshwater ecosystems in Sudan. In Renewable and Sustainable Energy Reviews, Vol. 12 2066–2091.

Paulson, S., Gezon, L.L. & Watts, M. (2003). Locating the political in political ecology: An Introduction. Human Organization 62 (3): 205–217.

Plater, T. (1994). Forced migration and resettlement as a strategy for development: An analysis of implications based on a study of the New Halfa Scheme in eastern Sudan. University of Pennsylvania.

Robbins, P. (2004). Political Ecology: a critical introduction. Blackwell Publishing.

Salem-Murdock, M. (1989). Arabs and Nubians in New Halfa. A Study of Settlement and Irrigation. University of Utah Press, Salt Lake City.

Shazali, S. & Ahmed, A. (1999). Pastoral Land Tenure and Agricultural Expansion: Sudan and the Horn of Africa. Paper presented at the DFID workshop on Land Rights and Sustainable Development in sub-Saharan Africa, UK.

Sørbø, G. (1977). How to Survive Development: The Story of New Halfa. Development Studies and Research Centre, Faculty of Economic and Social Studies, University of Khartoum, Khartoum University Press, Sudan.

Sørbø, G. (1985). Tenants and Nomads in Eastern Sudan. A Study of Economic Adaptations in the New Halfa Scheme. Scandinavian Institute of African Studies, Uppsala.

Sørbø, G.(2012). Environment, climate and the Sudanese Conflict. In Sudan: North in the shadow of the South. Seminar report for the seminar on challenges and opportunities for peacebuilding in Sudan, held in March and April 2012 in Uppsala and Stockholm, Sweden.

Staddon, C. (1988). Managing Europe's water resources: twenty-first century challenges. Ashgate Publishing, England.

Swyngedouw, E. (2009). The political Economy and Political Ecology of the Hydrosocial Cycle. In Journal of Contemporary Water Research & Education Issue 142, pages 1–5, June 2009.

Taha, F. (2010). The History of the Nile Waters in the Sudan. In: The River Nile in the Post-Colonial Age. Conflict and Cooperation among the Nile Basin Countries. Ed. Tvedt, T. I.B. Tauris & Co. Ltd, New York.

UNDP Sudan (2013). UNDP/Sudan Overview <http://www.sd.undp.org/sudan%20overview.htm> 28.8.2013.

UNEP (2007). Sudan. Post-Conflict Environmental Assessment. United Nations Environment Programme. Nairobi, Kenya.

Woodhouse, P. (1988). The Green Revolution and Food Security in Africa: Issues in Research and Technology Development. Development Policy and Practice Research Group. Working Paper No. 10. Milton Keynes, UK. Open University.

World Bank (1975). Assault on World Poverty. John Hopkins University Press, Baltimore and London.

World Bank (1989). Annual Review of Evaluation Results. Washington, DC.

World Bank (1992). Project Completion Report. Sudan, New Halfa Irrigation Rehabilitation Project. Africa Regional Office, World Bank.

World Commission on Dams (2000). Dams and Development. Earthscan Publisher, London.

Yong Ooi Lin, C. (2008). Indigenous Peoples, Displacement through 'Development' and Rights Violations: the Case of the Orang Asli of Peninsular Malaysia. In Forced Displacement: Why Rights Matter. Ed. Grabska, K. & Mehta, L. Palgrave Macmillan, UK.

CURRENT AFRICAN ISSUES PUBLISHED BY THE INSTITUTE

Recent issues in the series are available electronically for download free of charge www.nai.uu.se

1981

1. *South Africa, the West and the Frontline States. Report from a Seminar.*
2. Maja Naur, *Social and Organisational Change in Libya.*
3. *Peasants and Agricultural Production in Africa. A Nordic Research Seminar. Follow-up Reports and Discussions.*

1985

4. Ray Bush & S. Kibble, *Destabilisation in Southern Africa, an Overview.*
5. Bertil Egerö, *Mozambique and the Southern African Struggle for Liberation.*

1986

6. Carol B. Thompson, *Regional Economic Polic under Crisis Condition. Southern African Development.*

1989

7. Inge Tvedten, *The War in Angola, Internal Conditions for Peace and Recovery.*
8. Patrick Wilmot, *Nigeria's Southern Africa Policy 1960–1988.*

1990

9. Jonathan Baker, *Perestroika for Ethiopia: In Search of the End of the Rainbow?*
10. Horace Campbell, *The Siege of Cuito Cuanavale.*

1991

11. Maria Bongartz, *The Civil War in Somalia. Its genesis and dynamics.*
12. Shadrack B.O. Gutto, *Human and People's Rights in Africa. Myths, Realities and Prospects.*
13. Said Chikhi, Algeria. *From Mass Rebellion to Workers' Protest.*
14. Bertil Odén, *Namibia's Economic Links to South Africa.*

1992

15. Cervenka Zdenek, *African National Congress Meets Eastern Europe. A Dialogue on Common Experiences.*

1993

16. Diallo Garba, *Mauritania–The Other Apartheid?*

1994

17. Zdenek Cervenka and Colin Legum, *Can National Dialogue Break the Power of Terror in Burundi?*
18. Erik Nordberg and Uno Winblad, *Urban Environmental Health and Hygiene in Sub-Saharan Africa.*

1996

19. Chris Dunton and Mai Palmberg, *Human Rights and Homosexuality in Southern Africa.*

1998

20. Georges Nzongola-Ntalaja, *From Zaire to the Democratic Republic of the Congo.*

1999

21. Filip Reyntjens, *Talking or Fighting? Political Evolution in Rwanda and Burundi, 1998–1999.*
22. Herbert Weiss, *War and Peace in the Democratic Republic of the Congo.*

2000

23. Filip Reyntjens, *Small States in an Unstable Region – Rwanda and Burundi, 1999–2000.*

2001

24. Filip Reyntjens, *Again at the Crossroads: Rwanda and Burundi, 2000–2001.*
25. Henning Melber, *The New African Initiative and the African Union. A Preliminary Assessment and Documentation.*

2003

26. Dahilon Yassin Mohamoda, *Nile Basin Cooperation. A Review of the Literature.*

2004

27. Henning Melber (ed.), *Media, Public Discourse and Political Contestation in Zimbabwe.*

28. Georges Nzongola-Ntalaja, *From Zaire to the Democratic Republic of the Congo.* (Second and Revised Edition)

2005

29. Henning Melber (ed.), *Trade, Development, Cooperation – What Future for Africa?*
30. Kaniye S.A. Ebeku, *The Succession of Faure Gnassingbe to the Togolese Presidency – An International Law Perspective.*
31. J.V. Lazarus, C. Christiansen, L. Rosendal Østergaard, L.A. Richey, Models for Life – Advancing antiretroviral therapy in sub-Saharan Africa.

2006

32. Charles Manga Fombad & Zein Kebonang, *AU, NEPAD and the APRM – Democratisation Efforts Explored.* (Ed. H. Melber.)
33. P.P. Leite, C. Olsson, M. Schöldtz, T. Shelley, P. Wrange, H. Corell and K. Scheele, *The Western Sahara Conflict – The Role of Natural Resources in Decolonization.* (Ed. Claes Olsson)

2007

34. Jassey, Katja and Stella Nyanzi, *How to Be a "Proper" Woman in the Times of HIV and AIDS.*
35. M. Lee, H. Melber, S. Naidu and I. Taylor, *China in Africa.* (Compiled by Henning Melber)
36. Nathaniel King, *Conflict as Integration. Youth Aspiration to Personhood in the Teleology of Sierra Leone's 'Senseless War'.*

2008

37. Aderanti Adepoju, *Migration in sub-Saharan Africa.*
38. Bo Malmberg, *Demography and the development potential of sub-Saharan Africa.*
39. Johan Holmberg, *Natural resources in sub-Saharan Africa: Assets and vulnerabilities.*
40. Arne Bigsten and Dick Durevall, *The African economy and its role in the world economy.*
41. Fantu Cheru, *Africa's development in the 21st century: Reshaping the research agenda.*

2009

42. Dan Kuwali, *Persuasive Prevention. Towards a Principle for Implementing Article 4(h) and R2P by the African Union.*
43. Daniel Volman, *China, India, Russia and the United States. The Scramble for African Oil and the Militarization of the Continent.*

2010

44. Mats Hårsmar, *Understanding Poverty in Africa? A Navigation through Disputed Concepts, Data and Terrains.*

2011

45. Sam Maghimbi, Razack B. Lokina and Mathew A. Senga, *The Agrarian Question in Tanzania? A State of the Art Paper.*
46. William Minter, *African Migration, Global Inequalities, and Human Rights. Connecting the Dots.*
47. Musa Abutudu and Dauda Garuba, *Natural Resource Governance and EITI Implementation in Nigeria.*
48. Ilda Lindell, *Transnational Activism Networks and Gendered Gatekeeping. Negotiating Gender in an African Association of Informal Workers.*

2012

49. Terje Oestigaard, *Water Scarcity and Food Security along the Nile. Politics, population increase and climate change.*
50. David Ross Olanya, *From Global Land Grabbing for Biofuels to Acquisitions of AfricanWater for Commercial Agriculture.*

2013

51. Gessesse Dessie, *Favouring a Demonised Plant. Khat and Ethiopian smallholder enterprise.*

52. Boima Tucker, *Musical Violence. Gangsta Rap and Politics in Sierra Leone.*
53. David Nilsson, *Sweden-Norway at the Berlin Conference 1884–85. History, national identity-making and Sweden's relations with Africa.*
54. Pamela K. Mbabazi, *The Oil Industry in Uganda; A Blessing in Disquise or an all Too Familiar Curse? Paper presented at the Claude Ake Memorial Lecture.*
55. Måns Fellesson & Paula Mählck, *Academics on the Move. Mobility and Institutional Change in the Swedish Development Support to Research Capacity Buildiing in Mozambique.*
56. Clementina Amankwaah. *Election-Related Violence: The Case of Ghana.*
57. Farida Mahgoub. *Current Status of Agriculture and Future Challenges in Sudan.*
58. Emy Lindberg. *Youth and the Labour Market in Liberia – on history, state structures and spheres of informalities.*
59. Marianna Wallin. *Resettled for Development. The Case of New Halfa Agricultural Scheme, Sudan.*